D1451260

ATM, Volume II

Prentice Hall Series In
Advanced Communications Technologies

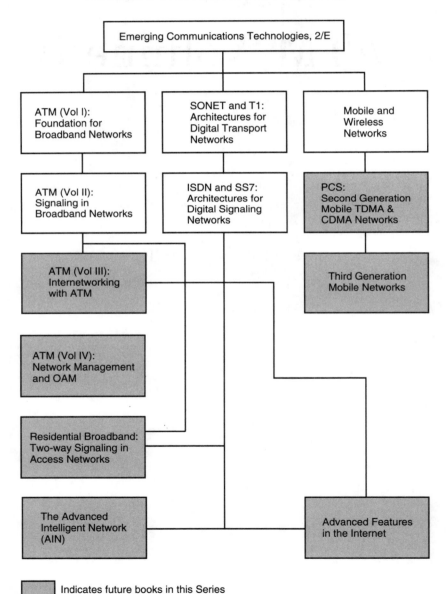

Emerging Communications Technologies, 2/E

ATM (Vol I):
Foundation for
Broadband Networks

SONET and T1:
Architectures for
Digital Transport
Networks

Mobile and
Wireless
Networks

ATM (Vol II):
Signaling in
Broadband Networks

ISDN and SS7:
Architectures for
Digital Signaling
Networks

PCS:
Second Generation
Mobile TDMA &
CDMA Networks

ATM (Vol III):
Internetworking
with ATM

Third Generation
Mobile Networks

ATM (Vol IV):
Network Management
and OAM

Residential Broadband:
Two-way Signaling in
Access Networks

The Advanced
Intelligent Network
(AIN)

Advanced Features
in the Internet

Indicates future books in this Series

ATM, Volume II
SIGNALING IN BROADBAND NETWORKS

UYLESS BLACK

To join a Prentice Hall PTR Internet mailing list, point to:
http://www.prenhall.com/mail_lists/

Prentice Hall PTR
Upper Saddle River, New Jersey 07458

Library of Congress Cataloging-in-Publication Data

Black, Uyless D.
    ATM—foundation for broadband networks / Uyless Black.
      p. cm.
    Includes bibliographical references and index.
    ISBN 0–13–571837–6
    1. Asynchronous transfer mode.   2. Broadband communication
systems. I Title.
    TK5105.35.B53   1995
    621.382—dc20   95–5961
                                          CIP

Acquisitions editor: Mary Franz
Cover designer: Scott Weiss
Cover design director: Jerry Votta
Manufacturing manager: Alexis R. Heydt
Marketing manager: Miles Williams
Compositor/Production services: Pine Tree Composition, Inc.

 Published by Prentice Hall PTR
Prentice-Hall, Inc.
A Simon & Schuster Company
Upper Saddle River, New Jersey 07458

Prentice Hall books are widely-used by corporations and government agencies for training, marketing, and resale.

The publisher offers discounts on this book when ordered in bulk quantities. For more information contact:

        Corporate Sales Department
        Phone: 800–382–3419
        Fax: 201–236–7141
        E-mail: corpsales@prenhall.com

        Or write:

        Prentice Hall PTR
        Corp. Sales Dept.
        One Lake Street
        Upper Saddle River, New Jersey 07458

Printed in the United States of America
10 9 8 7 6 5 4 3 2

ISBN: 0-13-571837-6

Prentice-Hall International (UK) Limited, *London*
Prentice-Hall of Australia Pty. Limited, *Sydney*
Prentice-Hall Canada Inc., *Toronto*
Prentice-Hall Hispanoamericana, S.A., *Mexico*
Prentice-Hall of India Private Limited, *New Delhi*
Prentice-Hall of Japan, Inc., *Tokyo*
Simon & Schuster Asia Pte. Ltd., *Singapore*
Editora Prentice-Hall do Brasil, Ltda., *Rio de Janeiro*

*This book is dedicated to my good friend
and goddaughter Holly Gillen*

During the time that I was writing this book about communications and signaling in broadband networks, I happened to watch a film about dolphins. The film demonstrated how dolphins communicate among themselves with certain types of audible signals, and how they use different signals for selected purposes such as location detection and mating rituals.

I was taken by the nature of their communication signals. At times they seemed to send digital "clicks"—something like the binary pulses employed by modern computer-based networks. At other times, they emitted different audible signals similar to the squeal of a high-pitched analog whistle. In a remarkable display of communications versatility, they alternated between transmitting "digital" and "analog" signals depending upon the occasion. These capabilities are performed by human-made systems with great difficulty and awkwardness (for example, the Digital AMPS technology).

Upon further study, I discovered that the digital clicks are also used as sonar signals and through a process called echolocation, dolphins can navigate and stay aware of their location and surroundings (something like our use of the global positioning system [GPS]).

Some researchers even claim that dolphins can use their signals to stun or kill a prey of another species with an acoustic shock (something like our use of a boom box on our own species).

The dolphins are quite social and scientists state that they possess an intelligence level far above most other mammals. They are said to be great imitators and some can imitate parts of human speech.

But in the final analysis, it is we humans who are the imitators. For time and time again, we find that our human creations and inventions are antedated by the natural world, in this case, the dolphin.

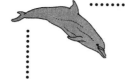

Contents

Preface   xv

CHAPTER 1   Introduction   **1**

Introduction   1
Purpose of a Signaling System   1
Transport Systems and Signaling Systems   2
    The Blurring of the Distinction between Transport
      and Signaling Networks   3
Narrowband Signaling Transport and Networks   3
    The T1 System   3
    X.25 and Packet Switching Systems   4
    SS7 Systems   6
    Problems with Narrowband Signaling   6
Broadband Signaling Networks   6
Why Not Just Use SS7?   7
Summary   7

CHAPTER 2   ISDN and B-ISDN Architecture   **8**

Introduction   8
Interfaces and Functional Groupings   8

Reference Points   10
ISDN Logical Channel Concept   11
Typical ISDN Configuration   12
The ISDN Layers   13
What Is B-ISDN?   14
B-ISDN Functional Entities and Reference Points   16
The B-ISDN Planes and Layers   16
Major Functions of the Layers   18
Classification of Broadband Services   21
Summary   23

CHAPTER 3   **ATM Architecture**   **24**

Introduction   24
ATM Architecture   24
Why the Interest in ATM?   26
ATM and B-ISDN   26
The ATM Layers   27
Virtual Circuits with the VPCI, VPI, and VCI   29
Virtual Path Connection Identifier (VPCI)   32
The ATM Cell and Cell Header   32
A Closer Look at AAL   34
Formats of the AAL PDUs   36
Summary   38

CHAPTER 4   **Signaling System Number 7 (SS7) Architecture**   **39**

Introduction   39
Early Signaling   39
Common Channel Signaling   40
SS7 Fundamentals   40
Example of an SS7 Topology   41
Functions of the SS7 Nodes   41
The Service Switching Point (SSP)   43
The Signaling Transfer Point (STP)   43
The Service Control Point (SCP)   43
The SS7 Levels (Layers)   44
SS7 Identifiers and Numbering Scheme   47
Global Title Addressing and Translation   49
Summary   49

CHAPTER 5   **Addressing, SAPs, Primitives, and PDUs**   **50**

Introduction   50
Explicit Addresses and Labels   50
A Short Treatise on Routing   51
The ATM Address Scheme   52
The E.164 Address Scheme   55
Service Access Points (SAPS)   56
    How Primitives (Service Definitions) Are Used   57
    Relationships of Service Definitions and Protocol
        Specifications   58
Connection Mapping   58
Other Key Concepts   60
ATM's Use of the OSI Model   60
The Broadband Signaling Stacks and the User Layers   60
Summary   63

CHAPTER 6   **SAAL, SSCOP, and SSCF**   **64**

Introduction   64
Position of SAAL in the Broadband Signaling Layers   64
    The Protocol Stack in More Detail   65
Functions of SAAL   67
    Functions of SSCF   67
    Functions of SSCOP   69
    Functions of SSCS Layer Management (LM)   70
The SAAL Primitives and Signals Operations   71
    Depictions of the Layers and Their Associated Primitives
        and Signals   72
    Primitives and Signals between SSCF and MTP 3   72
    Signals between SSCOP-SSCF and SSCOP-Layer
        Management   76
    Signals between Layer Management and SSCF   77
Signals between SSCOP and CPCS   78
The Error Codes   79
The SSCOP Operations in More Detail   79
    SSCOP PDUs   80
    Examples of SSCOP "Housekeeping" Operations   83
    Examples of SSCOP Transferring Signaling Traffic   84
Relationships of the SAAL Entities and MTP 3   89
    Parameters in the Primitives and PDUs   90

Summary   91

CHAPTER 7   **UNI Signaling**   92

Introduction   92
Broadband Signaling Stacks   92
UNI Messages and Information Elements   93
    Message Format   94
    The Messages   95
    The Information Elements (IEs)   95
Overview of UNI Operations   95
    The Q.2931 Timers   98
The UNI Operations in More Detail   100
    The Connection Establishment Operation   100
    The Connection Release Operation   101
    The Restart Operation   102
    The Status Inquiry Operation   103
    The Add Party Operation   103
    The Drop Party Operation   106
The Q.931 Message Information Elements in More
    Detail   106
    AAL Information Element   107
    Broadband Low Layer Information Element   109
ATM Forum UNI Version 4.0 Variations   112
Summary   112

CHAPTER 8   **B-ISUP Signaling**   113

Introduction   113
Purpose of B-ISUP   114
What B-ISUP Does Not Do   114
    Bandwidth Analysis and Path Discovery   115
Position of B-ISUP in the Broadband Signaling Layers   116
The SS7 MTP Support to B-ISUP   116
Overview of the B-ISUP Operations   117
    Trunk Groups and VPCIs   118
    Setting up the Virtual Circuits   119
B-ISUP NNI Messages and Parameters   119
    The Messages   120
    Parameters in the Messages   123
Examples of B-ISUP Operations   123
The B-ISUP Architecture in More Detail   127

Summary   130
Appendix 8A: Parameters Used in B-ISUP Messages   130
Appendix 8B: B-ISUP Interfaces, Primitives, and Primitive
    Parameters   138

CHAPTER 9   **Operations Between UNI and NNI**   **144**

Introduction   144
Typical Call Setup and Release Operations   144
Mapping between the UNI and NNI Messages
    and Information Elements   147
Summary   147

CHAPTER 10   **Other Broadband Signaling Operations
             and Performance Requirements**   **148**

Introduction   148
Configuration Options   148
Point-to-Multipoint Calls   152
Signaling Identifiers (SIDs)   152
    Add Party Operations   154
Performance Requirements for the Signaling Virtual Channel
    Connection (VCC)   155
Summary   158

CHAPTER 11   **Private Network–Network Interface (PNNI)**   **159**

Introduction   159
Why Another NNI Protocol?   159
Overview of PNNI Protocol   160
Unique Aspects of PNNI Signaling vis-à-vis Q.2931   161
PNNI Signaling Specification Model   162
Terms and Concepts   163
PNNI Metrics   165
    Metric Aggregation   167
Horizontal and Outside Links   171
PNNI Hierarchy Example   172
PNNI Signaling Messages   175
    A Look at the SETUP Message Information
        Elements   175
    PNNI Available Bit Rate (ABR) Descriptors   177

Designated Transit List (DTL)   178
Soft Permanent Virtual Connection Procedures   178
        Crank Back   179
        Designated Transit List   179
Information Elements for the Support of Other Services   179
Summary   179

Abbreviations   180
References   183
Index   187

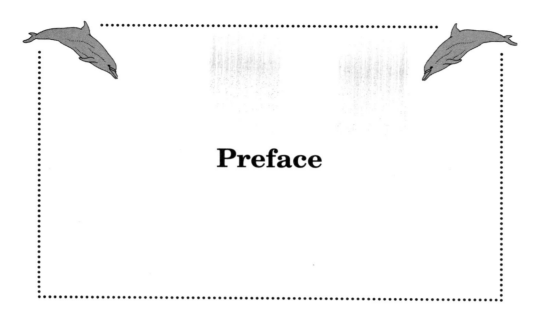

Preface

This book is one in a series of books called *Advanced Communications Technologies*. It is a companion book to *ATM: Foundation for Broadband Networks*. In the first volume, a chapter was devoted to ATM-based signaling operations at the UNI. Since the publication of that book, there has been an increased interest in the industry in signaling, both at the user-network interface (UNI) and the network-network interface (NNI). In addition, most of the specifications that define broadband signaling have now been released, and were not available when I wrote Volume I.

This book is written in response to the general interest of the public and provides a detailed description of the broadband signaling specifications. As the name of Volume I implies, ATM serves as a foundation for broadband networks. These broadband networks may or may not use signaling techniques in their operations, but the term broadband signaling does imply the use of signaling operations in a broadband network.

A separate book in this series is devoted to "narrow band signaling" and it is titled, *ISDN and SS7, Architectures for Digital Signaling Networks*. While this book is a useful reference guide when reading the book you have in your hands, I have included enough tutorial information in *ATM, Volume II* for you to deal with narrowband signaling. I also provided comparisons of narrowband and broadband signaling in this book.

I hope you find this book a valuable addition to your library and I hope you find it fulfills your needs. You can reach me at:

102732.3535@compuserve.com.

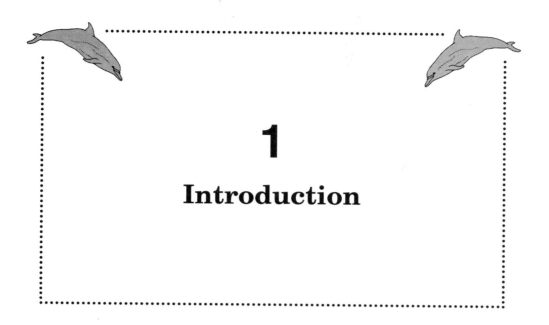

1

Introduction

INTRODUCTION

This chapter introduces the concept of a signaling system and compares a signaling system with a transport system. Early signaling systems are explained and compared to current systems (which are the focus of this book). Narrowband signaling systems are defined and are compared to broadband signaling systems. We also examine the role of the Asynchronous Transfer Mode (ATM) and Signaling System Number 7 (SS7) in broadband signaling networks.

PURPOSE OF A SIGNALING SYSTEM

The purpose of a signaling system is to transfer control information (signaling units) between elements in a telecommunications network. The elements are switches, operations centers, and databases. This information includes signaling units (also called messages) to establish and terminate connections (e.g., a voice call, a data connection) and other information such as directory service and credit card messages.

Originally, signaling systems were designed to set up connections between telephone offices and customer premises equipment (CPE) in order to transport only voice traffic through a voice-oriented, analog network. Today, they are designed to set up connections between service provider offices and CPE in order to transport not only voice but video or data signals through either an analog or a digital network.

TRANSPORT SYSTEMS AND SIGNALING SYSTEMS

A transport system is different from a signaling system. A transport system provides the physical facilities over which the signaling system operates. For example, a transport system defines the physical channel and the electrical/optical nature of the signals that operate on the channel. Examples of transport systems are T1 and the Synchronous Optical Network (SONET).

A signaling system defines how the physical channels are used and how they are allocated and provisioned to fit the user's needs. Signaling networks possess traits that allow the provisioning of bandwidth (capacity) on the physical channels to meet varying user throughput and delay requirements.

Signaling systems allow a user to request the network to provide certain quality of service (QOS) features to the user. They also provide a means for the user to convey certain QOS information to another end user, which the signaling network may act upon or pass (as a courtesy) directly to another user.

Figure 1–1 shows the relationships of a signaling system and a transport system between two machines labeled A and B. The transport

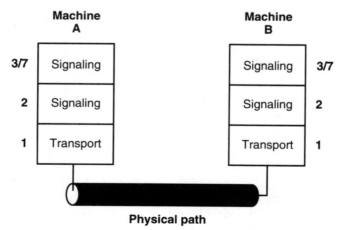

Physical path

Figure 1–1   Signaling and transport systems.

system operates at layer 1 of the layered model and the signaling system operates at layer 2 or perhaps layers 2 and 3, or layer 7.

The Blurring of the Distinction between Transport and Signaling Networks

The distinction between transport and signaling networks may be blurred in some systems, because they may do some of both. For example, SONET is primarily a transport technology, but it does have some signaling capabilities, and the narrowband Integrated Services Digital Network (ISDN) exhibits both transport and signaling characteristics. I will clarify and amplify this point in later discussions.

NARROWBAND TRANSPORT AND SIGNALING NETWORKS

The T1 System

In 1962 the U.S. Bell System (as it was known in the predivestiture days) installed the first commercial digital voice system in Chicago, Illinois. The system was known as T1 and carried 24 voice channels over copper wire between Bell's telephone offices. (This book uses the terms T1 and DS1 synonmously.)

T1 is designed to act principally as a transport network. Its signaling capabilities are very few, and the provisioning of channels (in the original T1 networks) was a labor-intensive, manual operation in which cables, dip switches, and other hardware had to be altered each time a new or revised user requirement developed.

T1 was designed to support fairly modest requirements for user applications, at least when compared to modern applications' needs. For example, the T1 systems support a transfer rate of 1.544 Mbit/s, and 28 T1s (called T3) operate at approximately 45 Mbit/s. These bit transfer rates may seem high to the reader, but remember that a 45 Mbit/s transport system like T3 only supports 672 voice calls—a lot of T3s have to be in operation to support the public telephone network.

These systems are often called narrowband signaling networks due to their limited capacity, typically no greater than 1.544 Mbit/s or 2.048 Mbit/s.

The T1 systems were designed to set up physical circuits (connections) for a call between two parties. These circuits were provisioned through hardware registers and by apportioning a physical circuit (which is usually called a DS0 channel, with a bit rate of 64 kbit/s) or a part of a physical circuit capacity (part of the circuit's bandwidth) for a call. Once the bandwidth was set up, it was fixed and could not be used by anyone else, even though the original customer would not be using the bandwidth. These networks suffered from bandwidth waste, because of the rigid manner in which bandwidth is allocated. Expensive and time-consuming tasks were involved in modifying and reprovisioning the bandwidth on these earlier systems.

Increasingly, many applications require bandwidth only when sending and receiving information. The vast part of the 64 kbit/s DS0 channel is wasted with a typical user needing only a fraction of the 64 DS0 slice of bandwidth.

X.25 and Packet Switching Systems

In the early 1970s, another technology, called packet switching, was deployed to support data networks. Unlike the T1 networks, which were designed for voice applications, packet switching networks have become the foundation for the majority of data networks.

Unlike T1, packet switching has a more flexible way of allocating bandwidth to users. First, bandwidth is not charged on a fixed basis; a user pays for what is used. Second, bandwidth need not be "nailed-up"; it can be allocated on a more dynamic basis to meet the varying needs of the user. And third, the network has more flexibility in managing bandwidth for all users and can make better use of network resources. Most of the functions came through the use of software to support user requirements instead of the T1 focus on hardware. Experience demonstrates that packet switched systems can be engineered to support up to eight times as many data users on the same T1 channel.

At about the same time that packet switching networks were being deployed, the International Telecommunications Union-Telecommunication Standardization Sector (ITU-T, formerly, the CCITT) published the X.25 specification. X.25 defines the procedures for user computers to communicate with network machines (packet switches) to transport data to another user computer. X.25 has become a widely used industry standard and has facilitated the building of standardized communications interfaces between different vendors' machines.

X.25 was designed for data systems that operate at only a few bit/s or a few hundred bit/s—typically 600 to 9600 bit/s. Although X.25 can be placed on very high-speed media and can operate efficiently at high speed, a substantial amount of subscriber equipment and software has been designed for modest transfer rates—typically no greater than 19.2 kbit/s.

Once again, sending data at a rate of 19.2 kbit/s may seem fast. After all, it translates to a transfer rate of 2400 characters per second (19,200/8 bits per character), and no one can type in an E-mail message that fast. However, for other applications, this speed is not sufficient. File transfers, database updates, and color graphics (to mention a few) need much greater transfer rates.

X.25 does have powerful signaling capabilities. A wide variety of signaling messages can be exchanged between network nodes and user devices to allocate, manage, and deallocate channel capacity for the user.

The Virtual Circuit Concept.   In comparison to T1, X.25 uses a different approach in its operations, called a virtual circuit (as opposed to a physical circuit). The term virtual circuit is used to describe a shared circuit (or circuits) wherein the sharing is transparent to the circuit users. The term was derived from computer architecture (in the 1960s) in which an end user perceives that a computer has more memory than actually exists and the capacity is shared by other users. The idea of a virtual circuit is to allow the bandwidth of physical circuits to be shared on a more flexible basis than what is available in a conventional physical circuit arrangement.

Inband and Out-of-Band Signaling.   Another aspect of X.25 is noteworthy: inband signaling. With this approach, signaling and user traffic share the same physical channel, with part of the channel capacity used for signaling traffic and the remainder of the bandwidth allocated for user traffic. Thus, signaling traffic and user traffic compete with each other for the channel capacity. In contrast, out-of-band signaling employs a separate physical channel for signaling.

Fixed and Variable Length Messages.   The X.25 signaling messages that are sent on the channel are variable length. The size of the message can range from 16 octets to 4096 octets; T1 uses fixed length messages (called frames). With fixed length units, transmission delay is more predictable as is queuing delay (if any) inside the switches. In addition, fixed length buffers are easier to manage than variable length buffers. In essence, a fixed-length system is more deterministic than the use of a technology with variable length data units.[1]

---

[1]There are also several disadvantages to the use of fixed-sized messages, but for this discussion the issue is moot, since broadband signaling is based partly on ATM, which uses fixed length units called cells. The first volume (*ATM: Foundation for Broadband Networks*) on ATM in this series examines this issue in more detail.

SS7 Systems

Newer signaling systems such as SS7 are classified as out-of-band signaling systems because they use a separate channel for signaling information. These systems are also called common channel signaling (CCS) systems because a shared (common) channel is used for signaling. SS7 is designed to be a pure signaling system and provides no features for a transport system. It relies on a transport system such as T1 or SONET to support the signaling services.

Problems with Narrowband Signaling

Some of the systems just described are quite specialized: As examples, T1 is designed for circuit-switched systems and X.25 is designed for packet-switched systems. This approach results in duplicate signaling systems, which is an expensive approach.

The older circuit-switched T1 systems provision bandwidth and do not allow it to be shared. Packet-switched systems are more flexible, but they are designed for data traffic only. Moreover, X.25 introduces considerable delay in the network because it is designed to perform extensive error-checking and editing operations on the traffic.

BROADBAND SIGNALING NETWORKS

A better approach is to combine some of the attractive characteristics of circuit switching, packet switching, and common channel signaling, and that is exactly what broadband signaling networks are designed to do. Their principal characteristics are:

- The provisioning of virtual circuits onto physical circuits to allow a more efficient allocation of network bandwidth.
- The use of out-of-band signaling channels, which translates into a more reliable system and ensures that critical signaling messages are delivered safely across the signaling link between the exchanges.
- Provisioning operations are performed more in software and less in hardware, which, again, provides more flexibility and leads to a more responsive reaction to user requirements and changes.
- The provisioned bandwidth can be accessed (borrowed) by other users (bandwidth is furnished dynamically to another user if one user is not using it).

- Provisioned bandwidth can be asymmetrical; that is, different bandwidth in each direction on the circuit. This feature is attractive for client-server applications wherein one end of the connection sends more traffic than the other end.
- The underlying technology is based on fixed length ATM cells.

This last statement warrants a few more comments. From the perspective of most of the telecommunications standards groups and telecommunications providers, ATM acts as the switching, multiplexing, and virtual circuit mechanism for broadband signaling networks. Technically, nothing precludes the use of other non-ATM options, but the broadband signaling systems that are described in this book allocate virtual circuits based on ATM virtual circuit concepts (for example, the fields in an ATM cell header) and ATM-based bandwidth requirements (for example, sustained and peak cell rate requirements for the virtual circuit).

WHY NOT JUST USE SS7?

Since SS7 is a very powerful and flexible signaling system, why not use it for broadband signaling? The answer is that SS7 is used and is an important part of a broadband signaling system. However, the original SS7 specification is designed for setting up, managing, and tearing down *physical* circuits (or parts of a physical circuit; e.g., a DS0 slot in a DS1 channel). It has no provisions for setting up, managing, and tearing down *virtual* circuits. To support broadband signaling, SS7 is modified to support not only virtual circuits but the operations that are associated with the ATM technology as well.

SUMMARY

Originally, signaling systems were designed to set up physical circuits (connections) between users. Narrowband signaling systems set up fixed slots (DS0 channels) with symmetrical bandwidth of 64 kbit/s in each direction.

Broadband signaling systems still set up connections, but the bandwidth can vary depending upon the individual needs of each user. These connections are based on ATM virtual circuits.

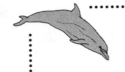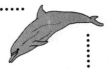

2

ISDN and B-ISDN Architecture

INTRODUCTION

This chapter provides an overview of the Integrated Services Digital Network (ISDN) and Broadband ISDN (B-ISDN) architectures. For detailed information on ISDN, the reader should refer to *ISDN and SS7: Foundation for Digital Signaling Networks*, published as part of this series. The emphasis in this chapter is B-ISDN.

Reference points and functional groups are explained with examples of typical implementations. ISDN logical and physical channels are introduced, as well as the ISDN and B-ISDN logical channels. A review is provided of the ITU-T view of B-ISDN services and the layers that comprise B-ISDN.

INTERFACES AND FUNCTIONAL GROUPINGS

An end user device connects to an ISDN node through a user network interface (UNI protocol) (see Figure 2–1). The UNI provides a connection to the network node (a switch, multiplexer, and the like), that can then support the user traffic flow through a network. At a remote UNI, the process is reversed, with the user traffic presented to the destination user across the UNI.

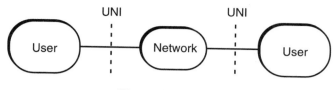

Figure 2–1   The UNI.

Two definitions are in order (and refer to Figure 2–2). Functional groupings are a set of capabilities needed in an ISDN user-access interface. Specific functions within a functional grouping may be performed by multiple pieces of equipment or software. Second, reference points are the interfaces dividing the functional groupings. Usually, a reference point corresponds to a physical interface between pieces of equipment. The reference point also defines the protocol that runs between the functional groupings.

The reference points labeled R, S, T, and U are logical interfaces between the functional groupings, which can be either a terminal equipment (TE) type 1, a terminal equipment type 2, or a network termination (NT) grouping. One other purpose of the reference points is to delineate where the responsibility of the network operator ends or begins.

The U reference point is the reference point for the 2-wire side of the NT1 equipment. It separates a NT1 from the line termination (LT) equipment. The U interface is a national standard, while interfaces implemented at reference points S and T are international standards. The R reference point represents non-ISDN interfaces, such as RS-422 and V.35.

The end-user ISDN terminal is identified by the ISDN term TE1. The TE1 connects to the ISDN through a twisted pair 4-wire digital link. The TE2 connects to a terminal adapter (TA), which is a device that allows non-ISDN terminals to operate over ISDN lines. The TA and TE2 devices are connected to either an ISDN NT1 or NT2 device. The NT1 is a device that connects the 4-wire subscriber wiring to the conventional 2-wire local loop. ISDN allows up to eight terminal devices to be addressed by NT1. The NT1 is responsible for the physical layer functions, such as signaling synchronization and timing. NT1 provides a user with a standardized interface.

The NT2 is a more intelligent piece of equipment. It may be found in a digital PBX and contains the layer 2 and 3 protocol functions. It can multiplex 23 B+D channels onto the line at a combined rate of 1.544 Mbit/s or 31 B+D channels at a combined rate of 2.048 Mbit/s.

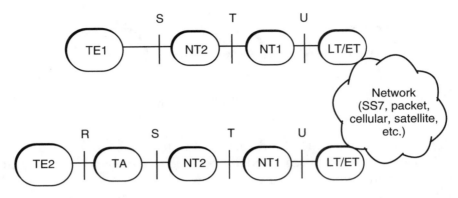

where:
 ET Exchange termination
 LT Line termination
 NT Network termination
 TA Terminal adapter
 TE Terminal equipment

Figure 2–2   ISDN model: Interfaces and functional groupings.

Reference Points

Figure 2–3 provides another view of the ISDN reference points. The purpose of the reference points is to define (1) the mechanical connectors, (2) the electrical signals, and (3) the procedures (protocols) that take place between the functional groupings. The S and T reference points are standardized internationally, and the U reference point is based on national standards within countries.

Depending on national or vendor implementations, network provider responsibilities end at the S, T, or U reference points:

> **1.** At the S reference point, the network provider is responsible for NT2 and NT1

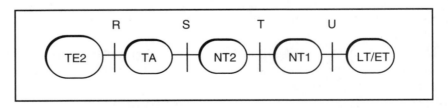

Figure 2–3   Reference points.

2. At reference point T, the network provider is responsible for NT1 only

3. At reference point U, the network provider is responsible for neither NT1 or NT2.

The S and T reference points may be the same (combined) if functional group NT2 is not implemented (that is, no NT2 is used, known as zero NT2). For this arrangement, reference point S operates at reference point T.

The R reference point defines conventional interfaces, such as the ITU-T V Series Recommendations, EIA-232-E, RS-442, and so on. As shown in this figure, the R reference point delineates the boundary between the non-ISDN world and the ISDN world.

ISDN LOGICAL CHANNEL CONCEPT

ISDN employs time division multiplexing (TDM) operations on its physical channels. The TDM slots contain user traffic (such as a voice signal, data signal, etc.), or control traffic (such as a call setup, network management message, etc.). These slots are structured in accordance with concise rules to keep the traffic on the physical channel organized into discrete, identifiable signals. This approach is quite important, because it enables the receiving machine to discern the type of traffic in each of the received slots and react accordingly.

As depicted in Figure 2–4, each slot is part of a "logical channel" that resides on the physical channel. The term logical channel is used to convey the idea of a logical association of TDM slots. On the physical media, the slots are discrete binary 1s and 0s. For ISDN, these slots are called D or B channels.

The B channel is similar to the DS0 slot in a DS1 (T1) system. As a general practice, the B channel at the UNI is mapped into a corresponding DS0 slot for transport across a higher capacity DS1 link. The mapping occurs at the customer premise equipment (CPE) if the customer subscribes to a primary rate (1.544 Mbit/s), or at the central office if the customer subscribes to a basic rate (64 kbit/s).

Each D channel is used to carry control/signaling information or user data. The B channels carry user voice, video, or data traffic. As shown in the figure, a D channel can operate at 16 or 64 kbit/s. In most commercial ISDN deployments, the D channel has not been made available to the end user; it is there but the customer cannot access it.

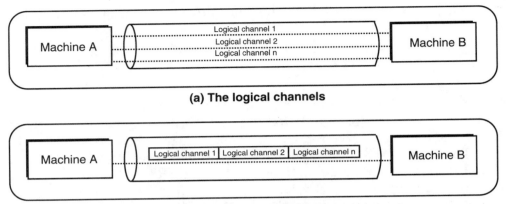

(a) The logical channels

(b) The logical channels on the physical channel

Examples:
- D Channel: 16 or 64 kbit/s
- B Channel: 64 kbit/s
- H Channel: Aggregates of B channels
      H0: 384 kbit/s (6 B channels)
      H11: 1536 kbit/s (24 B channels)
      H12: 1920 kbit/s (30 B channels) etc.

Figure 2–4   ISDN logical channels.

   With the recent problems of obtaining bandwidth and connections from the local telephone exchange and the Internet Service Provider (ISP), some companies are re-examining this practice. Although 16 kbit/s is not a lot of bandwidth, it beats having no bandwidth at all.

   The B channel operates at 64 kbit/s, although a number of B channels can be aggregated together to provide a user application more transmission capacity. For example, an H0 channel is an aggregation of six B channels, and operates at 384 kbit/s. In North America, these aggregated B channels are known as Fractional T1.

TYPICAL ISDN CONFIGURATION

   The TE1 connects to the ISDN through a twisted pair 4-wire digital link (Figure 2–5). This link uses TDM to provide three channels, designated as the B, B and D channels (or 2 B+D). The B channels operate at a speed of 64 kbit/s; the D channel operates at 16 kbit/s. The 2 B+D is designated as the basic rate interface (BRI), and ISDN allows up to eight TE1s to share one 2 B+D link. The purpose of the B channels is to carry

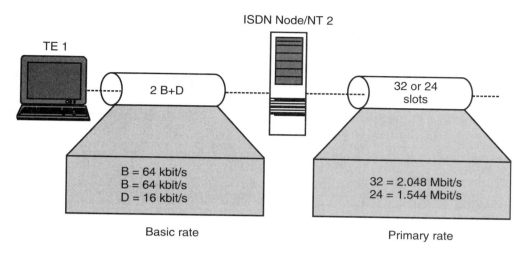

Figure 2–5   An ISDN configuration.

the user payload in the form of voice, compressed video, and data. The purpose of the D channel is to act as an out-of-band control channel for setting up, managing, and clearing the B channel connections.

In other configurations, the user DTE is called a TE2 device. As explained earlier, it is current equipment in use such as workstations and personal computers. The TE2 connects to a TA, which is a device that allows non-ISDN terminals to operate over ISDN lines. The user side of the TA typically uses a conventional physical layer interface such as EIA-232–D, RS-422 or the V-series specifications. It is packaged like an external modem or as a board that plugs into an expansion slot on the TE2 devices.

THE ISDN LAYERS

The ISDN approach is to provide an end user with full support through the seven layers of the OSI Model, although ISDN confines itself to defining the operations at layers 1, 2, and 3 of this model, as shown in Figure 2–6. In so doing, ISDN is divided into two kinds of services: the bearer services, responsible for providing support for the lower 3 layers of the seven-layer standard; and teleservices (for example, telephone, Teletex, Videotex message handling), responsible for providing support through all 7 layers of the model and generally making use of the underlying lower-layer capabilities of the bearer services. The services are referred to as low-layer and high-layer functions, respectively. The ISDN functions are allocated according to the layering principles of the OSI Model.

Figure 2–6 shows the ISDN layers. Layer 1 (the physical layer) uses either the basic rate interface (BRI) or 2 B+D, or the PRI, which is either 23 B+D or 31 B+D. These standards are published in ITU-T's I Series as I.430 and I.431, respectively. Layer 2 (the data link layer) consists of LAPD and is published in the ITU-T Recommendation Q.921. Layer 3 (the network layer), is defined in the ITU-T Recommendation Q.931.

WHAT IS B-ISDN?

B-ISDN cannot be described in one sentence. But it can be defined with a few definitions, numbered 1–9 in the following information.

1. B-ISDN's transfer rate on a communications link is anything beyond narrowband ISDN (N-ISDN). In other words, it is above the

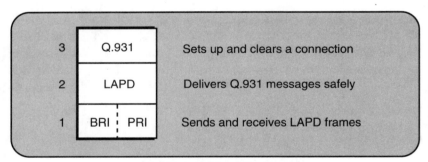

(a) Functions of the layers

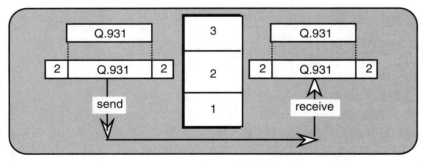

(b) Layer interaction

Figure 2–6   The ISDN layers.

1.544 Mbit/s and 2.048 Mbit/s rates of the N-ISDN primary rate. This declaration does not mean that B-ISDN does not use the lower rates, but the term "broadband" implies higher transfer rates. B-ISDN supports the lower rates as well.

2. B-ISDN continues to use the N-ISDN "model". Therefore, functional entities, reference points are used in all the B-ISDN specifications, but each is appended with a "B", to connote broadband. (See Figure 2–7 for an example of this notation.)

3. B-ISDN continues to use some of the N-ISDN protocols (with modifications), such as the N-ISDN layer three Q.931. This protocol is modified in B-ISDN to set up connections on demand (switched virtual calls [SVCs]) in an ATM network.

4. B-ISDN expands on the N-ISDN Model of layers and planes to accommodate full multiservice capabilities.

5. In a very broad context, B-ISDN describes the types of applications supported in a B-ISDN. A later discussion in this chapter expands on this idea.

6. The technical underpinnings of B-ISDN are ATM and SDH/SONET. They act as the bearer services to the applications that they support.

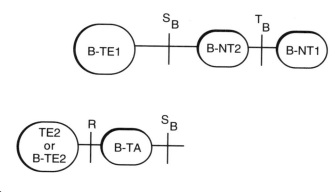

where:
    B   Broadband
    NT Network termination (ISDN devices)
    S/T ISDN reference points
    TA Terminal adapter (interfaces non-ISDN devices into ISDN interfaces)
    TE Terminal equipment (user devices)
        TE1 ISDN device
        TE2 Non-ISDN device

Figure 2–7   B-ISDN functional groups and reference points.

7. Provisioning of connections is performed on virtual circuits and not DS0 slots.

8. Bandwidth can be set up on a symmetrical or asymmetrical basis.

9. Bandwidth is provisioned on ATM performance parameters, such as peak cell rate, cell delay variation, ect.

B-ISDN FUNCTIONAL ENTITIES AND REFERENCE POINTS

In the early 1980s when ISDN standards were being established, the ITU-T concentrated on the H1 channel for the primary rate interface (PRI) and the 2 B+D interface for the basic rate interface (BRI). Interest shifted in the mid-1980s to higher speed channels due to the recognition of the need and the inadequacies of the BRI and PRI technologies. The various standards groups recognized the value of the architecture of ISDN and believed that higher capacity specifications could use the basic concepts of the work performed in the 1980s.

Thus, B-ISDN started out as an extension of ISDN and has many concepts similar to ISDN. For example, functional groupings still consist of TE1, TE2, NT1, NT2, and TA. Reference points are still R, S, and T. These are conveniently tagged with the letter B in front of them to connote the broadband architecture.

It should be emphasized that the similarities between ISDN and B-ISDN are only in concept and work well enough for a general model. In practice, the ISDN and B-ISDN interfaces are not compatible. It is impossible to upgrade an ISDN interface by simply supplementing it with B-ISDN functional groups and reference points. Therefore, the reader should consider these terms as abstract conceptions that are still useful for understanding the overall B-ISDN architecture.

Another point that should be noted is that most of the specifications (recommendations) developed by the ITU-T are written from the view of the network provider, and not the network user. This approach merely reflects the slant of the ITU-T, which, historically, has been to publish standards for use by public telecommunications operators (PTOs, such as AT&T, British Telecom, MCI, Sprint, etc.).

The B-ISDN Planes and Layers

The rather abstract view of B-ISDN and ATM can be viewed in a more pragmatic way. The three planes (control, user, and management)

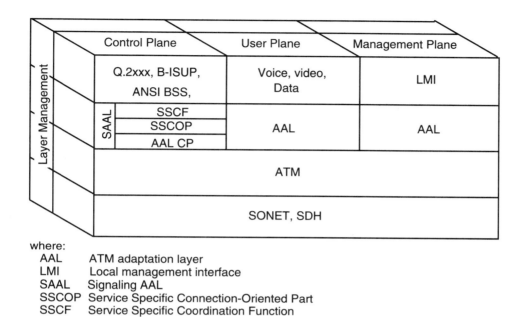

where:
AAL   ATM adaptation layer
LMI   Local management interface
SAAL   Signaling AAL
SSCOP   Service Specific Connection-Oriented Part
SSCF   Service Specific Coordination Function

Figure 2–8   Examples of protocol placement in the B-ISDN layers.

are shown in Figure 2–8 with the placements of protocols residing in the layers. Strictly speaking, the B-ISDN model defines SDH for the physical layer, although this figure shows other choices.

The ATM Adaptation Layer (AAL) is designed to support different types of applications and different types of traffic, such as voice, video, and data. The AAL plays a key role in the ability of an ATM network to support multi-application operations. It isolates the ATM layer from the myriad operations necessary to support diverse types of traffic. The ATM chapter will explain that AAL is divided into a convergence sublayer (CS) and a segmentation and reassembly sublayer (SAR). CS operations are tailored, depending on the type of application it is supporting. SAR operations entail the segmentation of payload into 48-octet SDUs at the originating SAR and reassembling the SDUs into the original payload at the receiver.

In the B-ISDN Signaling Model, the signaling AAL (SAAL) is designed to support the control plane. It is in this plane that the signaling operations take place

The ATM layer's primary responsibility is the management of the sending and receiving of cells between the user node and the network node. It adds and processes the 5-octet cell header.

The control plane contains the Q.2931 and B-ISDN signaling protocols that are used to set up connections in the ATM network (Q.2931 is a variation of Q.931). It also contains a variety of ITU-T X.2xxx Recommendations. The layer below Q.2931 is the signaling ATM adaptation layer (SAAL). SAAL contains three sublayers. Briefly, they provide the following functions. The AAL common part (AAL CP) detects corrupted traffic transported across any interface using the control plane procedures. The service-specific connection-oriented part (SSCOP) supports the transfer of variable length traffic across the interface and recovers from erred or lost service data units. The service-specific coordination function (SSCF) provides the interface to the next upper layer, in this case, Q.2931.

In the middle of Figure 2–8 is the user plane, which contains user- and applications-specific protocols, such as Transmission Control Protocol/Internet Protocol (TCP/IP) and the File Transfer Protocol (FTP). These protocols are chosen arbitrarily as examples of typical user protocols.

The management plane provides the required management services and is implemented with the ATM Local Management Interface (LMI). The Internet Simple Network Management Protocol (SNMP) and/or the OSI Common Management Information Protocol (CMIP) can also reside in the C-plane.

Figure 2–9 shows how the layers in the planes in the user machine communicate with the network machine or another user machine. The user device is represented by the stacks of layers on the left side of the figure, and the network node is represented by the stacks of the right side.

In accordance with conventional OSI concepts, each layer in the user machine communicates with its peer layer in the network node and vice versa. The one exception to this statement is at the U-plane. The ATM node (and ATM network) does not process the PDUs of the AAL and the user-specific protocols. This traffic is passed through the network to the corresponding peer layers on the remote side of the network. Once again, this concept is in the spirit of the OSI Model and its encapsulation/decapsulation techniques and the notion of the transparent aspect of a service data unit (SDU). To the ATM network, AAL and upper layer operations are SDUs.

MAJOR FUNCTIONS OF THE LAYERS

Figure 2–10 summarizes the ITU-T I.321 view of the major functions of the layers and sublayers of B-ISDN. The functions are listed on the left side of the figure, and the layers or sublayers in which the functions operate are shown in the right side of the figure.

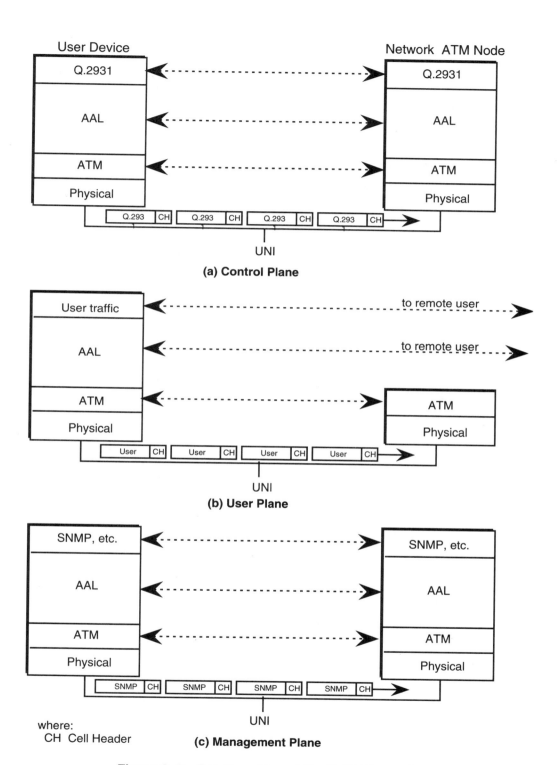

Figure 2–9   Relationships of the B-ISDN peer layers.

	Higher Layer Functions	Names of Higher Layers	
Layer Management	Convergence	CS	AAL
	Segmentation and reassembly	SAR	
	Generic flow control	ATM	
	Cell header processing		
	VPI/VCI processing		
	Cell muxing and demuxing		
	Cell rate decoupling	TC	PL
	HEC header processing		
	Cell delineation		
	Transmission frame adaptation		
	Transmission frame generation/recovery		
	Bit timing	PM	
	Physical medium		

where:
  AAL   ATM adaptation layer
  ATM   Asynchronous transfer mode
  CS   Convergence sublayer
  PL   Physical layer
  PM   Physical medium sublayer
  SAR   Segmentation and reassembly sublayer
  TC   Transmission convergence sublayer
  VPI   Virtual path identifier
  VCI   Virtual channel identifier

Figure 2–10   B-ISDN layer functions.

The physical layer (PL) contains two sublayers: the physical medium sublayer (PM) and the transmission convergence sublayer (TC). PM functions depend upon the exact nature of the medium (single mode fiber, microwave, etc.). It is responsible for typical physical layer functions, such as bit transfer/reception and bit synchronization. TC is responsible for conventional physical layer operations that are not medium dependent. It is organized into five major functions.

Transmission frame generation/recovery is responsible for the generation and recovery of PDUs. Transmission frame adaptation is responsible for placing and extracting the cell into and out of the physical layer frame. Cell delineation is responsible for the originating endpoint to define the cell boundaries in order for the receiving endpoint to recover all cells. Cell header processing is responsible for generating a header error check (HEC) field at the originating endpoint and processing it at the terminating endpoint in order to determine if the cell header has been damaged in transit. Cell rate decoupling inserts idle cells at the sending end and extracts them at the receiving end in order to adapt to the physical level bandwidth capacity.

The ATM layer is independent of the physical layer operations and, conceptually, does not care what medium an ATM cell is running on. The ATM layer is organized into four major functions.

Cell muxing and demuxing is responsible for multiplexing (combining) cells from various virtual connections at the originating endpoint and demultiplexing them at the terminating endpoint. VPI/VCI processing is responsible for processing the labels/identifiers in a cell header at each ATM node. ATM virtual connections are identified by a virtual path identifier (VPI) and a virtual channel identifier (VCI). Cell header processing creates the cell header (with the exception of the HEC field) at the originating endpoint and interprets/translates it at the terminating endpoint. The VPI/VCI may be translated into a SAP at this receiver. Generic flow control is responsible for creating the generic flow control field in the ATM header at the originator and acting upon it at the receiver.

The functions of the AAL, CS, and SAR were described earlier in this chapter.

CLASSIFICATION OF BROADBAND SERVICES

The ITU-T Recommendation I.211 describes the services offered by B-ISDN. The services are classified as either interactive services or distribution services. Interactive services, as the name implies, entail an ongoing dialogue between the service user and service provider. The distribution services also entail a dialogue between the service provider and service user but the dialogue is oriented toward a batch or remote job entry (RJE) basis.

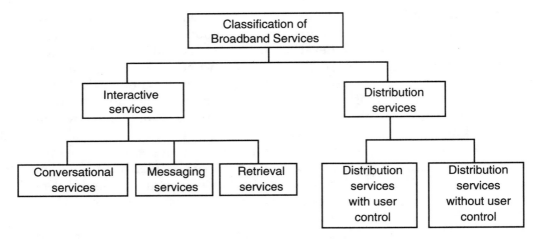

Figure 2–11   Classification of broadband services.

As depicted in Figure 2–11, interactive services are further classified as (1) conversational services, (2) messaging services, and (3) retrieval services. Distribution services are further classified as distribution services without user individual presentation control and distribution services with user individual presentation control.

Conversational services are interactive dialogues with real-time operations. In this context, real-time means that there are no store-and-forward operations occurring between the service user and service provider. For example, interactive teleshopping, ongoing message exchanges between two people, LAN-to-LAN communications, and building surveillance fall into the conversational services category.

Messaging services include user-to-user communications, such as video mail service or document mail service, which can be done on a conversational basis or on demand.

Retrieval services fall into the store-and-forward category where a user can obtain information stored for pubic use. This information can be retrieved on an individual basis from the service provider to the service user. Archival information is a good example of retrieval services.

Distribution services without user individual presentation control include conventional broadcast services such as television and radio. As the reader might expect, this service provides continuous flows of information where service users can obtain unlimited access to the information.

In contrast, distribution services with user individual presentation control allows the central source to distribute the information to a large or small number of users based on some type of cyclical repetition. Obviously, the B-ISDN category of interest here is the emerging video-on-demand market.

SUMMARY

ISDN is designed to be an all-digital user network interface (UNI). It is intended to be vendor and application independent. It supports user traffic on its B channels and allocates part of its bandwidth for signaling and control with its D channel. Through the use of TEIs and SAPIs, it can support and identify multiple workstations and applications within the workstations. And through the use of the terminal adapter (TA), it can support non-ISDN interfaces.

B-ISDN is based on the ISDN model, but is concerned with virtual circuits instead of DS0 slots. The B-ISDN virtual circuits are provisioned based on ATM performance parameters, such as peak rate, sustained cell rate, and cell delay variation.

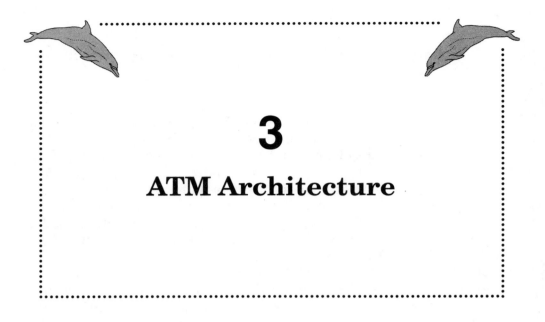

3

ATM Architecture

INTRODUCTION

This chapter provides an overview of the major functions of ATM networks. The initial part of the chapter describes how ATM supports different types of traffic and manages connections. The chapter also explains how ATM users are identified to the network through virtual connections.

ATM ARCHITECTURE

The Asynchronous Transfer Mode (ATM) forms the basis for many broadband networks, and it forms part of the foundation for B-ISDN networks. ATM uses multiplexing, switching, and segmentation/reassembly operations to support a high-speed transport network.

In an ATM network, all traffic is divided into small fixed-size units, called cells, and is sent over one channel and switched based on information in the cell header. The cell header contains two values, called the virtual path and virtual channel identifiers, which identify the cell to distinguish it unambiguously from other connections' cells.

ATM supports a multimedia environment; therefore, it must guarantee limits for delay and loss for different applications. It is also designed to exhibit high throughput and low delay by maximizing switch-

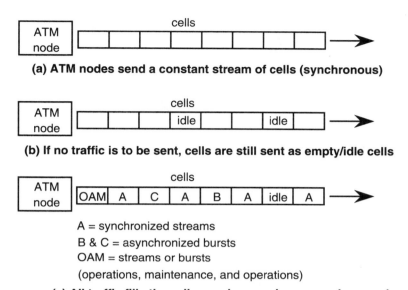

(a) ATM nodes send a constant stream of cells (synchronous)

(b) If no traffic is to be sent, cells are still sent as empty/idle cells

A = synchronized streams

B & C = asynchronized bursts

OAM = streams or bursts

(operations, maintenance, and operations)

(c) All traffic fills the cells synchronously or asynchronously

Figure 3–1   ATM transmission streams.

ing speed with the use of (1) short headers, (2) predefined paths, and (3) no link-to-link error recovery.

Newcomers to ATM often wonder why ATM has the term "asynchronous" as part of its title, especially since it supports synchronous traffic, such as voice and video applications. As depicted in Figure 3–1, the term is used because traffic is not necessarily assigned to fixed slots (cells) on the transmission channel, such as in a conventional time division multiplexing (TDM) system. Therefore, the cells of an application are not always in a fixed position in the channel. Because of this asynchronous aspect of the scheme, each cell must have a header attached to it that identifies each application's traffic in the cell stream. The scheme permits either synchronous or asynchronous allocation of the cells.

Even synchronous traffic, such as voice, can be placed into an ATM network in an asynchronous (bursty) fashion, as long as the receiving user machine "smooths" the asynchronous, bursty cell flow to a TDM-type presentation at the receiving application.

In Figure 3–1a, the ATM nodes send and receive a constant stream of cells. If the cells contain no traffic, they are identified as idle cells (Figure 3–1b). As stated previously, the cells can be filled either synchronously or asynchronously (as shown in Figure 3–1c).

WHY THE INTEREST IN ATM?

Without question, ATM has attracted considerable attention in the telecommunications industry. Other than the fact that new technologies attract articles in trade magazines, why has ATM drawn so much attention?

First, ATM is one of the few technologies that supports the transport of voice, video, and data applications over one media and one platform. Second, ATM is one of the few technologies to support LAN, WAN, and MAN traffic with one platform. It also allows a user to negotiate quality of service (QOS) features with the network, such as delay, CBR, VBR, ect.

ATM is designed to facilitate the implementation of many of these services in hardware, which translates to fast processing of all traffic and low delay through switches and networks.

ATM also allows a user to obtain scalable bandwidth and bandwidth on demand. A user need not be allocated fixed bandwidth, as in a time division multiplexed system. Since ATM does not define a specific port speed at the ATM and user devices, an ATM device can support different link speeds, and the switching fabric can be upgraded (made faster) as more devices (and/or more traffic) are added to the system. Lastly, ATM is a telecommunications transport technology that is a worldwide standard.

These statements are not meant to imply that other technologies are not designed to provide the same attractive services, but ATM offers an attractive combination of them.

ATM AND B-ISDN

ATM is designed for use with B-ISDN, which, in turn, is designed to support public networks. However, ATM can also be employed in private networks and therefore comes in two forms for the user-network interface (UNI):

- A public UNI defines the interface between a public service ATM network and a private ATM switch.
- A private UNI defines an ATM interface with an end user and a private ATM switch.

This distinction may seem somewhat superficial, but it is important because each interface will likely use different physical media and span different geographical distances.

It is obvious from a brief glance at Figure 3–2 that the ATM interfaces

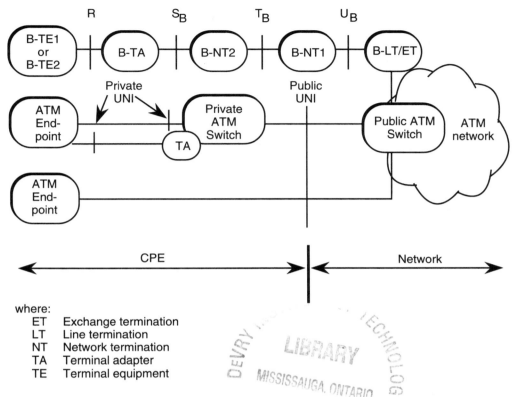

Figure 3–2 **Asynchronous Transfer Mode (ATM) B-ISDN model.**

where:
ET Exchange termination
LT Line termination
NT Network termination
TA Terminal adapter
TE Terminal equipment

and topology are organized around the ISDN model. As just stated, the UNI can be either public or private, and can span across S_B, T_B, and U_B interfaces. Internal adapters may or may not be involved. If they are involved, a user device (the B-TE1 or B-TE2) is connected through the R reference point to the B-TA. B-NT2s and B-NT1s are also permitted at the interface, with B-NT2 considered to be part of the CPE. For purposes of simplicity, the picture shows only one side of an ATM network. The other side could be a mirror image of the side shown in the figure, or it could have variations of the interfaces and components shown in the figure.

THE ATM LAYERS

As depicted in Figure 3–3, ATM provides convergence functions at the ATM adaptation layer (AAL) for connection-oriented and connection-

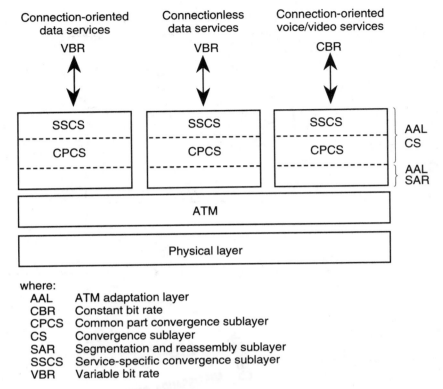

where:
AAL	ATM adaptation layer
CBR	Constant bit rate
CPCS	Common part convergence sublayer
CS	Convergence sublayer
SAR	Segmentation and reassembly sublayer
SSCS	Service-specific convergence sublayer
VBR	Variable bit rate

Figure 3–3   The ATM layers.

less variable bit rate (VBR) applications. It supports isochronous applications (voice, video) with constant bit rate (CBR) services.

A convenient way to think of the AAL is that it is actually divided into two sublayers, as shown in Figure 3–3. The segmentation and reassembly (SAR) sublayer, as the name implies, is responsible for processing user PDUs that are different in size and format into ATM cells at the sending site and reassembling the cells into the user-formatted PDUs at the receiving site. The other sublayer is called the convergence sublayer (CS), and its functions depend upon the type of traffic being processed by the AAL, such as voice, video, or data.

The SAR and CS entities provide standardized interfaces to the ATM layer. The ATM layer is then responsible for relaying and routing the traffic through the ATM switch. The ATM layer is connection-oriented and cells are associated with established virtual connections. Traffic must be segmented into cells by the AAL before the ATM layer can process the traffic. The switch uses the VPI/VCI label to identify the connection to which the cell is associated.

Broadband virtual private networks (VPNs) may or may not use the services of the ATM adaptation layer. The decision to use this service depends on the nature of the VPN traffic as it enters the ATM device.

The ATM layers do not map directly with the OSI layers. The ATM layer performs operations typically found in layers 2 and 3 of the OSI Model. The AAL combines features of layers 2 and 4 of the OSI Model. It is not a clean fit, but then, the OSI Model is over thirteen years old and it should be changed to reflect the emerging technologies.

The physical layer can be a SONET or SDH carrier. It may also be other carrier technologies, such as DS3, E3, or FDDI.

Whatever the implementation of AAL at the user device, the ATM network is not concerned with AAL operations for the ongoing processing of user traffic. Indeed, the ATM bearer service is "masked" from these CS and SAR functions. The ATM bearer service includes the ATM and physical layers. The bearer services are application independent, and AAL is tasked with accommodating to the requirements of different applications.

These ideas are amplified in Figure 3–4. For the transfer of user payload, upper layer protocols (ULP) and AAL operations are not invoked in the ATM network functions. The dotted arrows indicate that logical operations occur between peer layers at the user nodes and the ATM nodes. Therefore, the ULP headers, user payload, and the AAL headers are passed transparently through the ATM network. Of course, AAL must be invoked for the C-plane and M-plane because AAL must be available to assemble the payload in the cells back to an intelligible ULP PDU.

However, the bottom part of the figure shows that these upper layers are invoked by the network of SVC and OAM traffic. Whether the node inside the network invokes these layers depends upon the nature of the traffic. For example, if the traffic is a network management message between the user and its local node, then of course the "internal" network nodes will not participate in the operation.

VIRTUAL CIRCUITS WITH THE VPCI, VPI, AND VCI

Earlier discussions explained that an ATM connection is identified through two labels called the virtual path identifier (VPI) and virtual channel identifier (VCI). In each direction, at a given interface, different virtual paths are multiplexed by ATM onto a physical circuit. The VPIs and VCIs identify these multiplexed connections (see Figure 3–5).

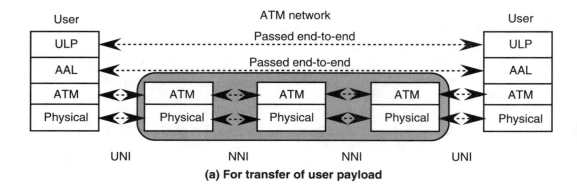

(a) For transfer of user payload

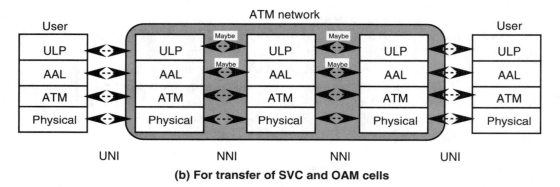

(b) For transfer of SVC and OAM cells

where:
   OAM   Operations, administration, and maintenance
   SVC   Switched virtual calls
   ULP   Upper layer protocols

Figure 3–4   Relationship of user and network layers.

Virtual channel connections can have end-to-end significance between two end users, usually between two AAL entities. The values of
these connection identifiers can change as the traffic is relayed through
the ATM network. For example, in a switched virtual connection, the
specific VCI value has no end-to-end significance. It is the responsibility
of the ATM network to "keep track" of the different VCI values as they
relate to each other on an end-to-end basis. Perhaps a good way to view
the relationship of VCIs and VPIs is to think that VCIs are part of VPIs;
they exist within the VPIs.

Routing in the ATM network is performed by the ATM switch exam-
ining both the VCI and VPI fields in the cell or only the VPI field. This

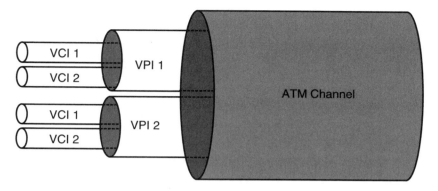

where:
VCI = Virtual channel identifiers
    VC link = terminated by points where VCI is assigned, translated or removed
VPI = Virtual path identifiers
    VP link = terminated by points where VPI is assigned, translated or removed

Figure 3–5   The ATM connection identifiers.

choice depends on how the switch is designed and if VCIs are terminated within the network.[1]

The VCI/VPI fields can be used with switched or nonswitched ATM operations. They can be used with point-to-point or point-to-multipoint operations. They can be pre-established (PVCs) or set up on demand, based on signaling procedures, such as the B-ISDN network layer protocol (Q.2931).

Additionally, the value assigned to the VCI at the user-network interface (UNI) can be assigned by the network, the user, or through a negotiation process between the network and the user.

To review briefly, the ATM layer has two multiplexing hierarchies: the virtual channel and the virtual path. The virtual path identifier (VPI) is a bundle of virtual channels. Each bundle must have the same end points. The purpose of the VPI is to identify a group of virtual channel (VC) connections. This approach allows VCIs to be "nailed-up" end-to-end to provide semi-permanent connections for the support of a large number of user sessions. VPIs and VCIs can also be established on demand.

---

[1]Some ATM implementations pass the VCI value unaltered through the network and use only the VPI to identify and switch the cell. The VCI is "fixed" and is transported transparently by the ATM network. This technique is called transparent VP service in the ATM Forum UNI specification (version 4.0). It is also known as VP switching.

The VC is used to identify a unidirectional facility for the transfer of the ATM traffic. The VCI is assigned at the time a VC session is activated in the ATM network. Routing might occur in an ATM network at the VC level, or VCs can be mapped through the network without further translation. If VCIs are used in the network, the ATM switch must translate the incoming VCI values into outgoing VCI values on the outgoing VC links. The VC links must be concatenated to form a full virtual channel connection (VCC). The VCCs are used for user-to-user, user-to-network, or network transfer of traffic.

The VPI identifies a group of VC links that share the same virtual path connection (VPC). The VPI value is assigned each time the VP is switched in the ATM network. Like the VC, the VP is unidirectional for the transfer of traffic between two contiguous ATM entities.

Referring to Figure 3–5, two different VCs that belong to different VPs at a particular interface are allowed to have the same VCI value (VCI 1, VCI 2). Consequently, the concatenation of VCI and VPI is necessary to uniquely identify a virtual connection.

Virtual Path Connection Identifier (VPCI)

The reader may have heard of or read about another label called the VPCI. It is used in broadband signaling, but the ATM layer is not concerned or aware of its presence (it is in another layer). The VPCI is explained in Chapter 5 (see the section entitled, "Virtual Path Connection Identifier [VPCI]").

THE ATM CELL AND CELL HEADER

The ATM PDU is called a cell (Figure 3–6). It is 53 octets in length, with 5 octets devoted to the ATM cell header and 48 octets used by AAL and the user payload. As shown in this figure, the ATM cell is configured slightly differently for the UNI than for the NNI. Since flow control and OAM operate at the UNI interface, a flow control field is defined for the traffic traversing this interface, but not at the NNI. The flow control field is called the generic flow control (GFC) field. If GFC is not used, this 4-bit field is set to zeros.

Most of the values in the 5-octet cell header consist of the virtual circuit labels of VPI and VCI. Most of the VPI and VCI overhead values are available to use as the network administrator chooses. Herein are some examples of how they can be used.

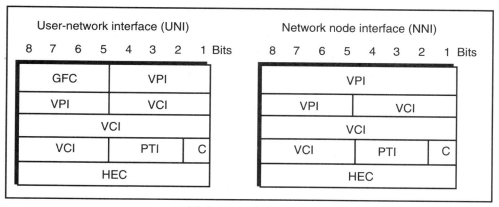

(a) A general view

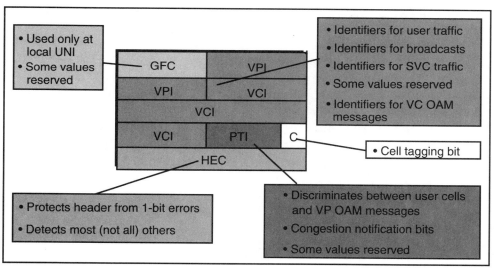

(b) A detailed view

where:
C: Cell loss priority
GFC: Generic flow control
HEC: Header error control
PTI: Payload type identifier
VCI: Virtual channel identifier
VPI: Virtual path identifier

Figure 3–6   The ATM protocol data units-PDUs (cells).

Multiple VCs can be associated with one VP. This approach can be used to assign a certain amount of bandwidth to a VP and then allocate it among the associated VCs. "Bundling" VCs in VPs allows one OAM message to be transmitted that provides information about multiple VCs, by using the VPI value in the header. Some implementations do not use all the bits of VPI/VCI to avoid processing all the bits in the VP and VC fields. Some implementations examine only the VPI bits at intermediate nodes in the network.

A payload type identifier (PTI) field identifies the type of traffic residing in the cell. The cell may contain user traffic or management/control traffic. The standards bodies have expanded the use of this field to identify other payload types (OAM, control, etc.). Interestingly, the GFC field does not contain the congestion notification codes, because the name of the field was created before all of its functions were identified. The flow control fields (actually, congestion notification bits) are contained in the PTI field.

The cell loss priority (C) field is a 1-bit value. If C is set to 1, the cell has a better chance of being discarded by the network. Whether the cell is discarded depends on network conditions and the policy of the network administrator. The field C set to 0 indicates a higher priority of the cell to the network.

The header error control (HEC) field is an error check field, which can also correct a 1-bit error. It is calculated on the 5-octet ATM header, and not on the 48-octet user payload. ATM employs an adaptive error detection/correction mechanism with the HEC. The transmitter calculates the HEC value on the first four octets of the header.

A CLOSER LOOK AT AAL

AAL is organized around a concept called service classes, which are summarized in Table 3–1. The classes are defined with regard to the following operations:

- Timing between sender and receiver (present or not present)
- Bit rate (variable or constant)
- Connectionless or connection-oriented sessions between sender and receiver
- Sequencing of user payload
- Flow control operations

Table 3–1 Support Operations for AAL Classes (Note: Work is underway to redefine AAL type 2)

Class	A	B	C	D
Timing	Synchronous	Scnchronous	Asynchronous	Asynchronous
Bit transfer	Constant	Variable	Variable	Variable
Connection mode	Connection-oriented	Connection-oriented	Connection-oriented	Connection-less
AAL type	1	2	3/4 and 5	3/4 and 5

- Accounting for user traffic
- Segmentation and reassembly (SAR) of user PDUs

As of this writing, the ITU-T had approved four classes, with labels of A through D. We will now summarize these classes and their major features. Table 3–1 summarizes the following thoughts.

Classes A and B require timing relationships between the source and destination. Therefore, clocking mechanisms are utilized for this traffic. ATM does not specify the type of synchronization—it could be a time stamp or a synchronous clock. This function is performed in the application running on top of AAL. Classes C and D do not require precise timing relationships. A constant bit rate (CBR) is required for class A, and a variable bit rate (VBR) is permitted for classes B, C, and D. Classes A, B, and C are connection-oriented, while class D is connection-less.

It is obvious that these classes are intended to support different types of user applications. For example, class A is designed to support a CBR requirement for high-quality video applications. On the other hand, class B, while connection-oriented, supports VBR applications and is applicable for VBR video and voice applications. For example, the class B service could be used by information retrieval services in which large amounts of video traffic are sent to the user and then delays occur as the user examines the information.

Class C services are the connection-oriented data transfer services such as X.25-type connections. Conventional connectionless services such as datagram networks are supported with class D services. Both of these classes also support (final decisions by ITU-T still pending) the multiplexing of multiple end users' traffic over one connection.

As of this writing, other classes are under study and undergoing revisions through ITU-T working groups. This work has been published in ITU-T Recommendation I.363 Annex 5.

Formats of the AAL PDUs

Figure 3–7 illustrates the formats of the AAL PDUs. AAL uses type 1 protocol data units (PDUs) to support applications requiring a constant bit rate transfer to and from the layer above AAL. It is also responsible for the following tasks:

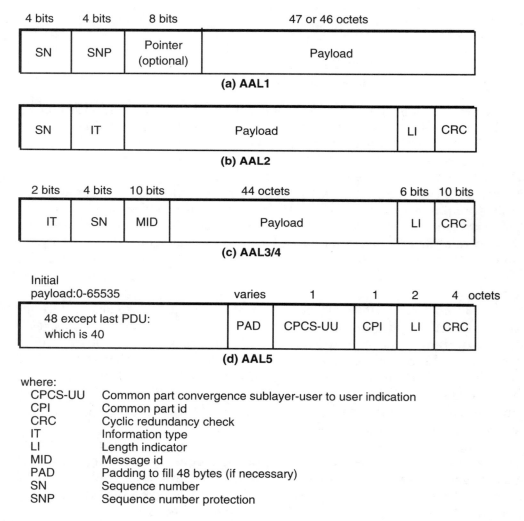

where:

CPCS-UU	Common part convergence sublayer-user to user indication
CPI	Common part id
CRC	Cyclic redundancy check
IT	Information type
LI	Length indicator
MID	Message id
PAD	Padding to fill 48 bytes (if necessary)
SN	Sequence number
SNP	Sequence number protection

Figure 3–7   The AAL PDUs.

1. Segmentation and reassembly of user information
2. Handling the variable cell delay
3. Detecting lost and mis-sequenced cells
4. Providing source clock frequency recovery at the receiver

The AAL1 PDU consists of 48 octets with 47 octets available for the user's payload. As shown in Figure 3–7a, the first header field is a sequence number (SN) and is used for detection of mistakenly inserted cells or lost cells. The other header field is the sequence number protection (SNP) that is used to provide for error detection and correction operations. AAL1 is responsible for clock recovery for both audio and video services.

AAL type 2 was designed for variable bit rate (VBR) services where a timing relationship is required between the source and destination sites. For example, class B traffic, such as variable bit rate audio or video, would fall into this category. This category of service requires that the timing information be maintained between the transmitting and receiving site. It is responsible for handling variable cell delay as well as the detection and handling of lost or missequenced cells.

The PDU for AAL2 consists of both a header and a trailer (see Figure 3–7b). The header consists of a sequence number (SN) as well as an information type (IT) field. The length of these fields and their exact functions have not been determined as of this writing. Obviously, the SN will be used for detection of lost and mistakenly inserted cells. The IT field can contain the indication of beginning of message (BOM), continuation of message (COM), or end of message (EOM). It may also contain timing information for audio or video signals.

The AAL2 trailer consists of a length indicator (LI) that is used to determine the number of octets residing in the payload field. Finally, the cyclic redundancy check (CRC) is used for error detection.

The original AAL2 has just been described. It has not been used, and as of this writing, work is underway to use AAL2 for multiplexing small packets over ATM.

The original ATM standards established AAL3 for VBR connection-oriented operations and AAL4 for VBR connectionless operations. These two types have been combined and are treated as one type. As the AAL standard has matured, it became evident that the original types were inappropriate. Therefore, AAL3 and AAL4 were combined due to their similarities and shown as AAL3/4.

As shown in Figure 3–7c, the AAL3/4 PDU carries 44 octets in the payload and 5 fields in the header and trailer. The 2-bit information type

(IT) is used to indicate the beginning of message (BOM), continuation of message (COM), end of message (EOM), or single segment message (SSM). The sequence number is used for sequencing the traffic. It is incremented by one for each PDU sent, and a state variable at the receiver indicates the next expected PDU. If the received SN is different from the state variable, the PDU is discarded. The message identification (MID) field is used to reassemble traffic on a given connection. The length indicator (LI) defines the size of the payload. Finally, the cyclic redundancy check (CRC) field is a 10-bit field used to determine if an error has occurred in any part of the cell.

AAL5 was conceived because AAL3/4 was considered to contain unnecessary overhead. It was judged that multiplexing could be handled by any upper layer, and that the operations to preallocate buffers at the receiver were not needed.

Figure 3–7d shows the format of the AAL5 PDU. It consists of an 8-octet trailer. The PAD field acts as a filler to fill out the PDU to 48 octets. The CPCS-UU field is used to identify the user payload. The common part indicator (CPI) has not been fully defined in ITU-T I.363. The length indicator (LI) field defines the payload length, and the CRC field is used to detect errors in the SSCS PDU (user data).

Type 5 is a convenient service for frame relay because it supports connection-oriented services. In essence, the frame relay user traffic is given to an ATM backbone network for transport to another frame relay user.

SUMMARY

ATM is a high-speed, low-delay, multiplexing and switching technology that supports any type of user traffic, such as voice, data, and video applications. ATM uses small, fixed-length units called cells that are identified with VPIs and VCIs that are contained in the cell header.

ATM provides limited error detection operations, provides no retransmission services, and few operations are performed on the small header. ATM also has a layer that operates above it, called the ATM adaptation layer (AAL), which performs convergence as well as segmentation and reassembly operations on different types of traffic.

4

Signaling System
Number 7 (SS7) Architecture

INTRODUCTION

This chapter introduces the Signaling System Number 7 network, known simply as SS7. The concepts behind the SS7 design are explained and SS7 nodes are examined. The relationship of SS7 and the OSI Model are clarified, as well as the SS7 topologies and link (communications channel) types. SS7 addresses are explained and we show some examples of these addresses. The chapter concludes with a discussion of internetworking and international SS7 networks.

EARLY SIGNALING

Early signaling systems used a technique called per-trunk, in-band signaling. With this approach, the call control path is the same physical circuit as the speech path. Consequently, call control competes with voice traffic for use of the channel. This is not an efficient technique, since the traffic of the telephone calls and the traffic of the control signals are competing with each other. Supervisory functions, such as on-hook and off-hook; call information, such as dial tone and busy signals; and addressing information, such as the called number, must be interspersed with the voice traffic.

COMMON CHANNEL SIGNALING

In contrast to per-trunk signaling, common channel signaling (CCS) divides the call control path from the speech path. As a consequence, call control does not compete with voice traffic for use of the channel. Moreover, this approach reduces call setup time and provides the opportunity to build redundant links between offices, which improves reliability. Another advantage of CCS is the ability to look ahead when setting up a connection. Therefore, resources do not have to be reserved until it is determined that a connection can be made. Thus, the high reliability coupled with faster operations and increased capabilities provide both local exchange carriers (LECs) and interchange carriers (ICs or IXCs) with a powerful tool for enhancing telephone operations.

There are two types of communications employed in common channel signaling, associated signaling and quasi-associated signaling. With associated signaling, common channel signaling messages pertaining to a particular operation are conveyed over communication links that are connected directly between the network nodes. With quasi-associated signaling, the messages are transferred indirectly through at least one tandem point usually known as the signaling transfer point (STP). Even though intermediate nodes are involved in the transfer of the messages, the messages always take a fixed, predetermined path between the two communicating entities.

SS7 FUNDAMENTALS

Common channel signaling (CCS) systems were designed in the 1950s and 1960s for analog networks and later adapted for digital telephone switches. In 1976, AT&T implemented the Common Channel Interoffice Signaling (CCIS) into its toll network. This system is referred to as CCS6 and was based on the CCITT Signaling System No. 6 Recommendation. SS6 and CCS6 were slow and designed to work on low bit rate channels. Moreover, these architectures were not layered, which made changing the code a complex and expensive task.

Consequently, the CCITT began work in the mid-1970s on a new generation signaling system. These efforts resulted in the publication of SS7 in 1980, with extensive improvements published in 1984 and again in 1988. Today, SS7 and variations are implemented throughout the world. Indeed, SS7 has found its way into other communications architectures such as personal communications services (PCS) and global systems for mobile communications (GSM).

SS7 defines the procedures for the setup, ongoing management, and clearing of a call between telephone users. It performs these functions by exchanging telephone control messages between the SS7 components that support the end users' connection.

The SS7 signaling data link is a full duplex, digital transmission channel operating at 64 kbit/s. Optionally, an analog link can be used with either 4 or 3 kHz spacing. The SS7 link operates on both terrestrial and satellite links. The actual digital signals on the link are derived from pulse code modulation (PCM) multiplexing equipment or from equipment that employs a frame structure. The link must be dedicated to SS7. In accordance with the idea of clear channel signaling, no other transmission can be transferred with these signaling messages.

EXAMPLE OF AN SS7 TOPOLOGY

Figure 4–1 depicts a typical SS7 topology. The subscriber lines are connected to the SS7 network through the service switching points (SSPs). The SSPs receive the signals from the CPE and perform call processing on behalf of the user. SSPs are implemented at end offices or access tandem devices. They serve as the source and destination for SS7 messages. In so doing, SSP initiates SS7 messages either to another SSP or to a signaling transfer point (STP).

FUNCTIONS OF THE SS7 NODES

SSP, STP, and service control points (SCP) are all SS7 nodes that are also known as signaling points. The STP is tasked with the translation of the SS7 messages and the routing of those messages between network nodes and databases. The STPs are switches that relay messages between SSPs and SCPs as well as other STPs. Their principal functions are similar to the layer 3 operations of the OSI Model.

The SCPs contain software and databases for the management of the call. For example, 800 services and routing are provided by the SCP. They receive traffic (typically requests for information) from SSPs via STPs and return responses (via STPs) based on the query.

Although Figure 4–1 shows the SS7 components as discrete entities, they are often implemented in an integrated fashion by a vendor's equip-

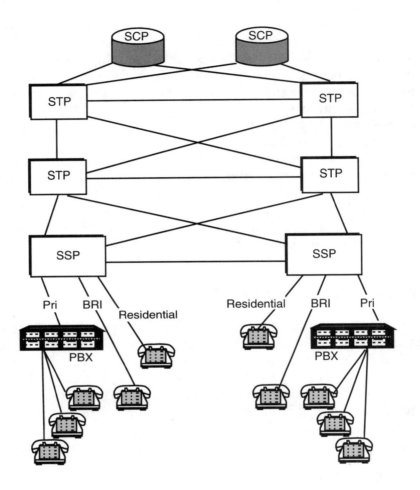

where:
BRI   Basic rate interface
PBX   Private branch exchange
PRI   Primary rate interface
SCP   Service control point
SSP   Service switching point
STP   Signaling transfer point

Figure 4–1   Example of an SS7 topology.

ment. For example, a central office can be configured with a SSP, a STP, and a SCP or any combination of these elements. These SS7 components are explained in more detail later in this section.

The Service Switching Point (SSP)

The SSP is the local exchange to the subscriber and the interface to the telephone network. It can be configured as a voice switch, an SS7 switch, or a computer connected to a switch.

The SSP creates SS7 signal units at the sending SSP and translates them at the receiving SSP. Therefore, it converts voice signaling into the SS7 signal units, and vice versa. It also supports database access queries for 800/900 numbers

The SSP uses the dialed telephone numbers to access a routing table to determine a next exchange and the outgoing trunk to reach this exchange. The SS7 connection request message is then sent to the next exchange.

The Signaling Transfer Point (STP)

The STP is a router for the SS7 network. It relays messages through the network but it does not originate them. It is usually an adjunct to a voice switch and does not usually stand alone as a separate machine.

The STP is installed as a national STP, an international STP, or a gateway STP. Even though SS7 is an international standard, countries may vary in how some of the features and options are implemented. The STP provides the conversions of the messages that flow between dissimilar systems. For example, in the United States the STP provides conversions between ANSI SS7 and ITU-T SS7.

STPs also offer screening services, such as security checks on incoming and/or outgoing messages. The STP can also screen messages to make certain they are acceptable (conformant) to the specific network.

Other STP functions include the acquisition and storage of traffic and usage statistics for OAM and billing. If necessary, the STP provides an originating SCP with the address of the destination SCP.

The Service Control Point (SCP)

The SCP acts as the interface into the telephone company databases. These databases contain information on the subscriber, 800/900 numbers, calling cards, fraud data, and so on. The SCP is usually linked to computer and/or databases through X.25. The SCP address is a point code, and the address of the database is a subsystem number (addresses are explained shortly).

The SS7 Levels (Layers)

Figure 4–2 shows the levels (layers) of SS7. The right part of the figure shows the approximate mapping of these layers to the OSI Model. Beginning from the lowest layers, the message transfer part (MTP) layer 1 defines the procedures for the signaling data link. It specifies the functional characteristics of the signaling links, the electrical attributes, and the connectors. Layer 1 provides for both digital and analog links al-

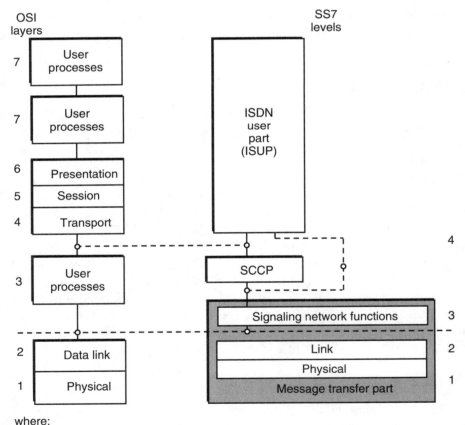

where:
   SCCP   Signaling connection control point

Figure 4–2   A general view of the SS7 levels (layers).

though the vast majority of SS7 physical layers are digital. The second layer is labeled MPT layer 2. It is responsible for the transfer of traffic between SS7 components. It is quite similar to an HDLC-type frame and indeed was derived from the HDLC specification. The MPT layer 3 is somewhat related to layer 3 of ISDN and X.25 in the sense that this layer provides the functions for network management, and the establishment of message routing as well as the provisions for passing the traffic to the SS7 components within the SS7 network. Many of the operations at this layer pertain to routing, such as route discovery and routing around problem areas in an SS7 network.

The signaling connection control point (SCCP) is also part of the network layer and provides for both connectionless and connection-oriented services. The main function of SCCP is to provide for translation of addresses, such as ISDN and telephone numbers to identifiers used by MTP 3 to route traffic.

The ISDN user part (ISUP) is responsible for transmitting call control information between SS7 network nodes. In essence, this is the call control protocol, in that ISUP sets up, coordinates, and takes down trunks within the SS7 network. It also provides features such call status checking, trunk management, trunk release, calling party number information, privacy indicators, detection of application of tones for busy conditions, and so on. ISUP works in conjunction with ISDN Q.931. Thus, ISUP translates Q.931 messages and maps them into appropriate ISUP messages for use in the SS7 network.

Figure 4-3 provides a more detailed description of the SS7 levels and will serve as an introduction to subsequent material on these levels. The three MTP levels serve as a connectionless transport system. With this approach, each SS7 message is routed separately from other messages, and there is no connection setup for the message transport.

MTP level 1 performs the functions of a traditional OSI physical layer. It generates and receives the signals on the physical channel. MTP level 2 relates closely to the OSI layer 2. It is a conventional data link level, and is responsible for the delivery of traffic on each link between SS7 nodes. The traffic in the upper layers of SS7 are encapsulated into MTP 2 "signal units" (this term is used by SS7 instead of the conventional HDLC "frame" term) and sent onto the channel to the receiving node. This node checks for errors that may have occurred during transmission and, if necessary, takes remedial action (discussed later).

MTP 3 is the connectionless routing part of the MTP levels. MTP level 3 performs OSI layer 3 functions, notably, the routing of messages between machine and between components within a machine. It per-

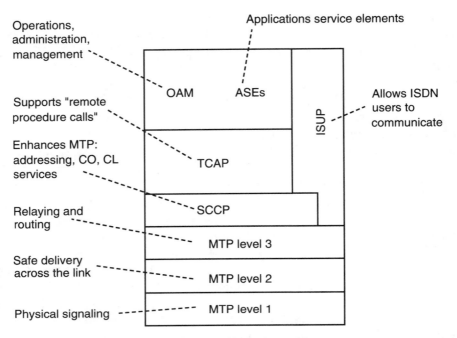

Operations, administration, management

Applications service elements

Supports "remote procedure calls"

Enhances MTP: addressing, CO, CL services

Relaying and routing

Safe delivery across the link

Physical signaling

OAM   ASEs

ISUP

Allows ISDN users to communicate

TCAP

SCCP

MTP level 3

MTP level 2

MTP level 1

Note: The terms level and layer are used interchangably.

where:
CL   Connectionless
CO   Connection-oriented
ISUP   ISDN user part
MTP   Message transfer part
SCCP   Signaling connection control point
TCAP   Transaction capabilities application part

Figure 4–3   The SS7 levels in more detail.

forms load-sharing operations across multiple links and reconfiguration operations in the event of node or link failure.

SCCP corresponds to several of the operations associated with OSI layer 3 (and although not generally discussed in literature, OSI layer 4, as well). Some of its principal jobs are: (1) supporting the MTP levels with global addressing, (2) providing connectionless or connection-oriented services, and (3) providing sequencing and flow-control operations.

The transaction capabilities application part (TCAP) corresponds to several of the functions of the OSI layer 7. It uses the remote operations service element (ROSE). As such, it performs connectionless, remote procedure calls on behalf of an "application" running on top of it.

The ISDN user part (ISUP) provides circuit-related services needed to support applications running in an ISDN environment. Non-ISDN originated calls are also supported by ISUP

The transaction capabilities application part (TCAP) is an OSI application layer. It can be used for a variety of purposes. One use of TCAP is the support of 800 numbers (in North America) that are transferred between SCP databases. It is also used to define the syntax between the various communicating components, and it uses a standard closely aligned with OSI transfer syntax, called the basic encoding rules (BER). Finally, the OMAP and ASEs are used respectively for network management and user-specific services.

SS7 IDENTIFIERS AND NUMBERING SCHEME

SS7 nodes (signaling points) are identified with an address and each node must have a unique address. The SS7 addresses are called point codes (PCs) or signaling point codes. The PC is kept transparent to entities operating outside the SS7 network; no direct correlation is made between a PC and a telephone number or an ISDN address. Any correlation between these identifiers is made by each network. The PC is placed inside the L_3 MTP message and used to route the message to the appropriate signaling point.

The PC is a hierarchical address consisting of (1) a network identifier, (2) a network cluster, and (3) a network cluster member. The network identifier, as its name implies, identifies a signaling network. The network cluster identifies a cluster of nodes that belong to a network. Typically, a cluster of signaling nodes consists of a group that home in on a mated pair of STPs. They can be addressed as a group. The network cluster member code identifies a single member (signaling point) operating within a cluster. The structure of the point code system and its relationship to signaling points is depicted in Figure 4–4. For example, a PC could be 123.2.4 to identify cluster member 4, which belongs to cluster 2, which belongs to network 123.

The structure of the PC fields is different in United States, ITU-T, and other national specifications. Each country may implement its own PC structure, but is expected to support an ITU-T structure at the international gateway (between two countries).

In addition to the PC used by MTP for routing to a node in the network, SS7 also utilizes a subsystem number (SSN). This number does not pertain to a node but to entities within a node, such as an application or

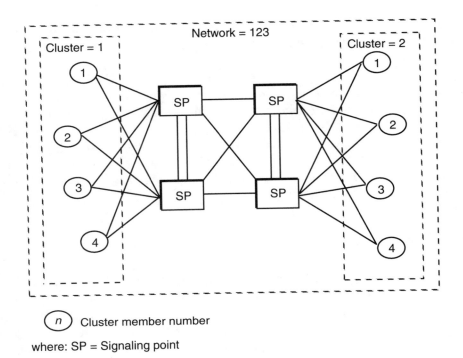

Figure 4–4   SS7 numbering plan.

some other software entity. As examples, it could identify enhanced 800 (E800) services running in a node, an automated calling card service (ACCS) module operating in the node, ISUP, and so on.

SS7 also supports the global title (GT) identifier, which could be the dialed digits of a telephone number. Perhaps the best way to view the GT is that it is mapped to an SS7 network address of PC + SSN.

As we shall see later, an SS7 subsystem operates as a user to SCCP. Therefore, SCCP "routes" traffic to and from the proper subsystem operating on top of SCCP.

The assignment of the codes is governed by each country's telecommunications administrations. The assignment scheme provides for three types of registration: (1) network code; (2) network code and cluster code; and (c) network code, cluster code, and cluster member codes, which is called a signaling point code block. For large networks, registration type (a) is used. Large networks must have more than 75 signaling points and 5 STPs in the first five years of operation, and several other requirements in outgoing years.

For small networks, registration type (b) is used. Registration type (c) is used for a group of signaling points that are not part of a network and have no STP.

Global Title Addressing and Translation

Obviously, the telephone user is not concerned with SS7 addresses. This customer need only enter a called party telephone number, and SS7 will set up the call. To the SS7 network, the telephone number is a global title, and as such, does not contain sufficient information for routing in the signaling network. Furthermore, a user may not use a conventional telephone number as a called address. Other identifiers may be used—as examples, 911 number, a mobile phone number, a telex number, or an 800 number.

SS7 is adaptable enough to accept these logical addresses and translate them to a routing address in order to support the call. Typically, an SS7 network contains sites that are responsible for these translations, and most systems place these operations at designated STPs. As we shall see in later discussions, SCCP is the SS7 entity that provides for global title translations.

SUMMARY

SS7 is the international standard for out-of-band signaling systems. Most systems in the world are quite similar, with some minor variations on a national or regional basis. Initially employed for use by the telephone network, SS7 is now used in mobile, wireless networks, and ATM networks, and broadband signaling networks.

5

Addressing, SAPs, Primitives, and PDUs

INTRODUCTION

This chapter examines the addresses and identifiers used in a broadband signaling network. Since the OSI Model plays a key role in this network, the subjects of service access points (SAPs), primitives, and protocol data units (PDUs) are also explained. We also compare addresses to labels (virtual circuit identifiers).

The only addresses used in ATM broadband signaling that are not discussed in this chapter are the SS7 point codes and global titles that are covered in Chapter 4.

EXPLICIT ADDRESSES AND LABELS

In order for the end user application's traffic to be sent to the proper destination (the terminating end point), a control field in the traffic must contain an identifier of the destination. If this identifier is not understood by a node that is supposed to relay it to the destination, the traffic cannot be delivered. Therefore, it is important that these identifiers be understood by all communicating parties: the originating party, the terminating party, and the network (and its switches). Most systems use one or two kinds of identifiers called explicit addresses or labels.

A specific address is one that has a location associated with it. As an example, the telephone numbering plan has a structure that permits the identification of a geographical region in the world, an area within that region, a telephone exchange within the area, and the telephone that is connected to the exchange. As another example, the CCITT X.121 has a structure that permits identification of a country, a network within that country, and a device within that network. Further values are used with these structures for applications running within the host, such as file servers and message servers. Explicit addresses are used by switches, routers, and bridges as an index to look up tables as to how to route the traffic.

Another identifying scheme is known by the term label although the reader may be more familiar with other terms such as logical channel number (LCN) or virtual circuit identifier (VCI). A label contains no information about network identifiers or locations. It is simply a value that is assigned to a user's traffic that identifies each data unit of that user's traffic.

The most common practice is to reserve a label such as a VCI for permanent virtual circuits (PVCs). This means that the user of the PVC need only submit to the network the label in the header associated with the user's traffic. The network then uses this label to examine tables to determine explicit location information. For a switched virtual call (SVC), also called connections on demand, the typical practice is to provide a label and an explicit address to the network, and this information is mapped into tables for the management of the ongoing call. Once this mapping has occurred, the user need only submit to the network the label, which is used as a lookup into a table to find an explicit address.

A SHORT TREATISE ON ROUTING

Upon receiving traffic from an incoming link, the network switch examines an address or a virtual circuit id in the traffic header and matches it with an entry in a routing table to determine where to route the traffic.

This routing decision is based on an entry in the routing table that identifies the next node (switch) in the path to the final destination. The switch then places the traffic onto the outgoing link that is attached to that next node. Upon receiving the traffic, this next switch goes through the same process, which is repeated until the traffic arrives at the terminating endpoint. Here, the traffic is passed to the destination application, through the use of other identifiers that distinguish which user application is to receive the traffic. These "other" identifiers are coded in the form of service access points (SAPs) and are explained later in this chapter. For this narration, the emphasis is on the identifiers that are used to route the traffic to the terminating end point.

THE ATM ADDRESS SCHEME

With connection on demand operations in ATM networks, it is important to have a standardized convention for coding destination and source addresses. Addressing is not an issue with PVCs since connections and endpoints (destination and source) are defined, and a user need only provide the network with a preallocated VCI/VPI. However, for SVCs, the destination connection can change with each session; therefore, explicit addresses are required. After the call has been mapped between the UNIs, the VCI/VPI values then can be used for traffic identification.

The ATM address is modeled on the OSI network service access point (NSAP), which is defined in ISO 8348 and ITU-T X.213, Annex A (Figure 5–1a). A brief explanation of the OSI NSAP and its relationship to ATM addressing follows.

The ISO and ITU-T describe a hierarchical structure for the NSAP address, as well as the structure for the NSAP address. It consists of four parts:

Initial Domain Part (IDP): Contains the authority format identifier (AFI) and the initial domain identifier (IDI).

Authority Format Identifier (AFI): Contains a 1-octet field to identify the domain specific part (DSP).

Initial Domain Identifier (IDI): Specifies the addressing domain and the network addressing authority for the DSP values; it is interpreted according to the AFI.

Domain Specific Part (DSP): Contains the address determined by the network authority; for ATM, the contents vary, depending on value of the AFI.

Figure 5–1b shows typical contents of the DSP. It can contain a variety of identifiers. It is used by ATM to identify a private or public address, as well as the end station, such as a user computer. It may also contain information on which protocols are to be invoked at the destination end station. Since a user device may be operating with different stacks of protocols, an SVC operation can identify which protocols are to receive the incoming traffic.

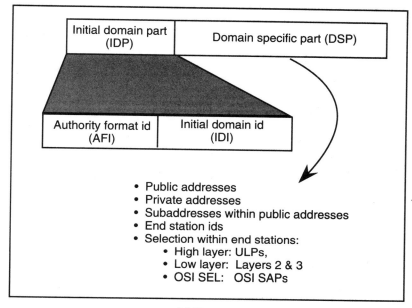

(a) Format

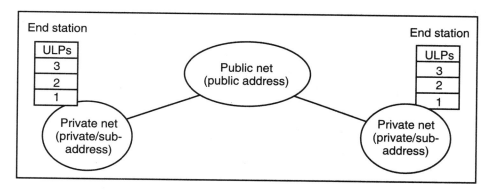

(b) Example

where:
SAPs   Service access points
ULPs   Upper layer protocols

Figure 5–1 The OSI address format.

Figure 5–2 shows the conventions for coding the OSI address for ATM operations. For ATM, the AFI field is coded as:

39 = DCC ATM format
47 = ICD ATM format
45 = E.164 format

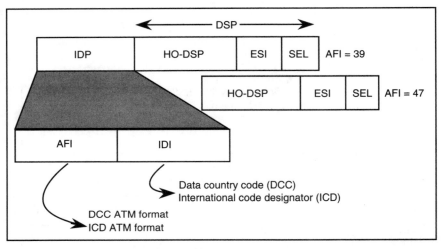

(a) Format for DCC and ICD Addresses

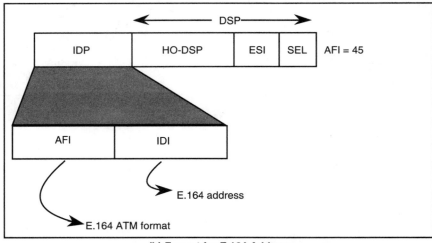

(b) Format for E.164 Address

Figure 5–2 The OSI/ATM address formats.

The IDI is interpreted according to the AFI (where AFI = 39, 47, or 45). For ATM, the IDI is coded as (1) a data country code (DCC) in accordance with ISO 3166; (2) the international code designator (ICD), which identifies an international organization and is maintained by the British Standards Institute; or (3) an E.164 address, which is a telephone number.

The domain specific part identifier (DFI) specifies the syntax and other aspects of the remainder of the DSP. The administrative authority (AA) is an organization assigned by the ISO that is responsible for the allocation of values in certain fields in the DSP. The R field is a reserved field.

The high-order DSP is established by the authority identified by the IDP. This field might contain a hierarchical address (with topological significance, see RFC 1237) such as a routing domain and areas within the domain. The end system identifier (ESI) identifies an end system (such as a computer) within the area.

The selector (SEL) is not used by an ATM network. It usually identifies the protocol entities in the upper layers of the user machine that are to receive the traffic. Therefore, the SEL could contain upper layer service access points (SAPs), which are explained shortly.

ATM public networks must support the E.164 address and private networks must support all formats. E.164 is covered in the next section of this chapter.

THE E.164 ADDRESS SCHEME

The ITU-T E.164 Recommendation is the prevalent standard for addresses in telecommunications systems throughout the world. E.164 is a variable length of decimal digits arranged in specific field. The fields are the country code (CC) and the national (significant) number (Figure 5–3).

The CC is used to select the destination country and varies in length as outlined in Recommendation E.163.

The national (significant) number N(S)N is used to select the destination subscriber. In selecting the destination subscriber, however, it may be necessary to select a destination network. To accomplish this selection, the N(S)N code field comprises a national destination code (NDC) followed by the subscribers number (SN).

The NDC field will be variable in length depending upon the requirements of the destination country. Each NDC may have one of the following structures:

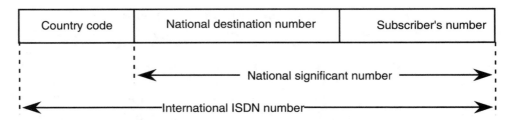

Figure 5–3 E.164.

1. A destination network (DN) code, which can be used to select a destination network serving the destination subscribers.
2. A trunk code (TC), the format of which is defined in Recommendation E.160.
3. Any combination of DN and TC.

The international number may be of variable length. The maximum number length shall be fifteen digits. However, some administrations may wish to increase their register capacity to sixteen or seventeen digits. The decision on register capacity is left to individual administrations.

The length does not include prefixes, language digit, address delimiters (e.g., end of pulsing signals, etc.) since these items are not considered as part of the international ISDN number.

SERVICE ACCESS POINTS (SAPS)

The services invoked at a layer are dictated by the upper layer's passing primitives (transactions) to the lower layer. In Figure 5–4, users A and B communicate with each other through a lower layer.

Services are provided from the lower layer to the upper layer through a service access point (SAP). The SAP is an identifier. It identifies the entity in layer N+1 that is performing the service(s) for layer N.

An entity in machine A can invoke some services in machine B through the use of SAPs. For example, a user that sends traffic can identify itself with a source SAP id (SSAP). It identifies the recipient of the traffic with a destination SAP value (DSAP).

It is the responsibility of the receiving lower layer N (in concert of course with the operating system in the receiving machine) to pass the traffic to the proper destination SAP in layer N+1. If multiple entities

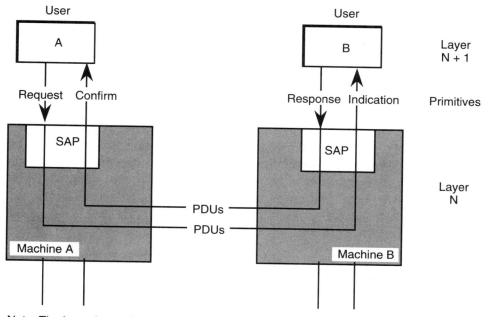

Note: The lower layers follow the identical procedures.

where:
  SAP Service access point

Figure 5-4   SAPs and primitives (service definitions).

(e.g., processes) exist in the machine, the DSAP serves to properly identify the process.

Some people view the SAP as a software "port." It is akin to the
socket concept found in the UNIX operating system environment.

How Primitives (Service Definitions) Are Used

The primitive is used by the layer to invoke the service entities and
create any headers that will be used by the peer layer in the remote station. This point is quite important. The primitives are received by adjacent layers in the local site and are used to create the headers used by
peer layers at the remote site. At the receiving site, the primitive is used
to convey the data to the next and adjacent upper layer and to inform
this layer about the actions of the lower layer.

The OSI Model uses four types of primitives to perform the actions
between the layers (Figure 5-4; Table 5-1. The manner in which they are
invoked varies. Not all four primitives must be invoked with each opera-

Table 5–1   Functions of Primitives

At user A:

- *Request*. A primitive initiated by a service user to invoke a function.
- *Confirm*. A primitive response by a service provider to complete a function previously invoked by a request primitive. It may or may not follow the response primitive.

At user B:

- *Indication*. A primitive issued by a service provider to (a) invoke a function, or (b) indicate a function has been invoked.
- *Response*. A primitive response by a service user to complete a function previously invoked by an indication primitive.

tion. For example, if the remote machine has no need to respond to the local machine, it need not return a response primitive. In this situation, a request primitive would be invoked at the local site to get the operation started. At the remote site, the indication primitive would be invoked to complete the process.

Of course, if the remote station were to send traffic back, it would invoke the operation with a response primitive, which would be mapped to the confirm primitive at the local machine.

Relationships of Service Definitions and Protocol Specifications

The ITU-T and ISO use two key terms in describing the OSI standards. This figure describes these terms as they relate to the material discussed in earlier parts of this chapter. In summary, they are:

- *Service Definitions*: Defines the services and operations that take place between the layers of the model within the same machine. The service definitions are implemented with primitives.
- *Protocol Specifications*: Actions taken within or between peer layers of the model across different machines (or two peer layers within the same machine) These actions taken are based on the service definitions.

CONNECTION MAPPING

The OSI Model specifies several procedures to manage connections between protocol entities. In Figure 5–5a, a direct or one-to-one mapping is shown. For this operation, one (N+1) connection is mapped directly to one (N) connection.

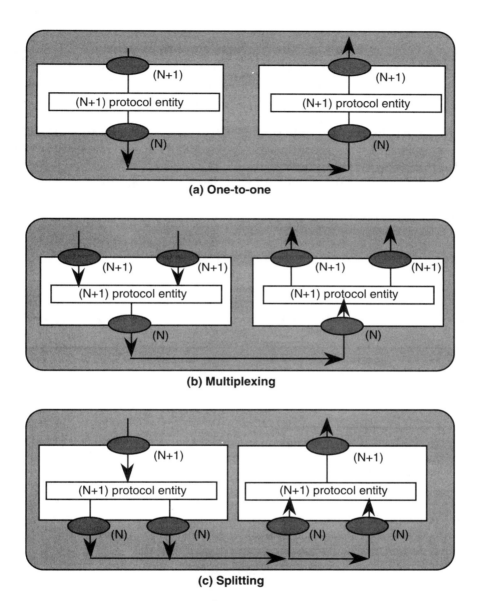

(a) One-to-one

(b) Multiplexing

(c) Splitting

Figure 5–5 Connection mapping.

In Figure 5–5b, the multiplexing of many-to-one connection mapping is shown. This is a common practice in the industry to mapping multiple users onto one network connection. If these users need the same quality of service from a network, and if they are connected to the same endpoint, one connection can be set up to manage all their connections.

This approach has several advantages. For example, it permits users (at the upper layers) to set up and tear down connections without requiring network intervention and provisioning. As another example, the network can signal OAM (operations, administration, and maintenance) to multiple users with one message that is identified with one SAP, and this signal is pertinent to multiple connections.

In Figure 5–5c, the splitting of one connection to multiple connections is also a useful function. For example, a user (upper layer) may need more bandwidth than is available on a single connection at a lower layer. The user can "fool" the lower layer (say, the network layer—representing the network itself), by obtaining multiple connections to improve the user's throughput.

OTHER KEY CONCEPTS

Figure 5–6 depicts the relationship of the layers from the standpoint of how data are exchanged between them. Three terms are important to this discussion.

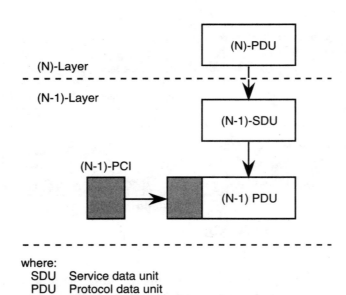

where:
    SDU   Service data unit
    PDU   Protocol data unit
    PCI   Protocol control information (headers and trailers)

Figure 5–6   Mapping between layers.

- *SDU (service data unit):* Consists of user data and control information created at the upper layers that is transferred transparently through a primitive by layer (N+1) to layer (N) and subsequently to (N-1). The SDU identity is preserved from one end of an (N)-connection to the other end.
- *PCI (protocol control information):* Information exchanged by peer (the same) entities at different sites on the network to instruct the peer entity to perform a service function (PCI is also called by these names: headers and trailers).
- *PDU (protocol data unit):* The PDU is a combination of the SDU and PCI.

This process repeats itself at each layer. At the transmitting site, the PDU becomes larger as it passes through each layer. At the receiving site, the PDU becomes smaller as it passes (up) through each layer.

ATM'S USE OF THE OSI MODEL

Figure 5–7 shows the conventions for the ATM and AAL layers, as well as the placement of service access points (SAPs) and the naming conventions.

This figure is largely self-explanatory. It can be seen that the naming conventions follow the OSI conventions and use the concepts of service data units (SDUs), protocol data units (PDUs), primitives, encapsulation, decapsulation, and protocol control information (PCIs).

THE BROADBAND SIGNALING STACKS AND THE USER LAYERS

To wrap up this chapter, Figure 5–8 shows how the layers of ATM and SDH/SONET relate to the user layer(s). We have learned that the layers communicate with each other between two machines through the use of PDUs. At the ATM layer, the PDUs are called cells; at the physical layer, the PDUs are called frames.

The service definitions define the interactions between adjacent layers in the same machine and use service access points (SAPs) to identify the source and destination communicating parties. The service definitions are known as primitives and are actually implemented with computer-specific operations, such as C function calls, UNIX system li-

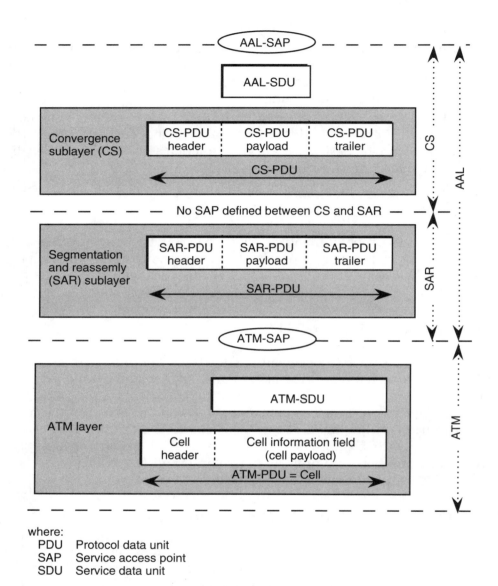

where:
PDU   Protocol data unit
SAP   Service access point
SDU   Service data unit

Figure 5–7   AAL general data unit conventions.

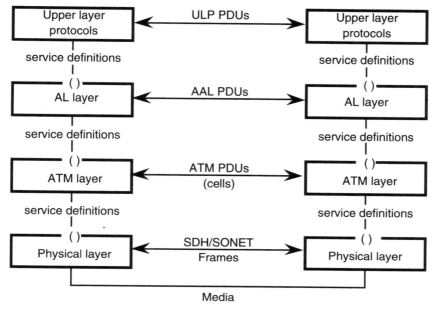

Note: ( ) represents a service access point (SAP)

Figure 5–8   Broadband signaling and the user layer(s).

brary calls, and so on. The user layer (or layers) rest on top of AAL and are known as upper layer protocols.

SUMMARY

ATM is organized into layers, SAPs, and service definitions, along the lines of the OSI Model. The SAPs and service definitions are a useful tool for designers and programmers, because they provide guidance on how to build the interfaces between the layers.

The use of OSI addresses is required in a broadband signaling network when a connection is requested by an ATM user. The ATM address can take several forms; the E.164 address is the most common form at this time.

6

SAAL, SSCOP, and SSCF

INTRODUCTION

This chapter examines the signaling ATM adaptation layer (SAAL) and its associated sublayers, the service-specific coordination function (SSCF), and the service-specific connection oriented protocol (SSCOP). The relationship of these entities to each other and to ATM layer management is also explored.

Since most of the interactions of SAAL entities within an exchange occur through primitives, an explanation is provided of the primitives' operations. The messages that are transferred between exchanges are explained and several examples are provided to show how SAAL services are used in the broadband signaling network.

Due to the many interfaces between SAAL and its upper and lower layers as well as those between the sublayers of SAAL and the many primitives and signals that are invoked between them, it is not practical to compare the differences between the ANSI and ITU-T specifications. For purposes of continuity and simplicity, I will explain the ANSI specifications.

POSITION OF SAAL IN THE BROADBAND SIGNALING LAYERS

Figure 6–1 compares the broadband signaling stacks (protocol stacks) for UNI and NNI operations and the placement of SAAL in these stacks.

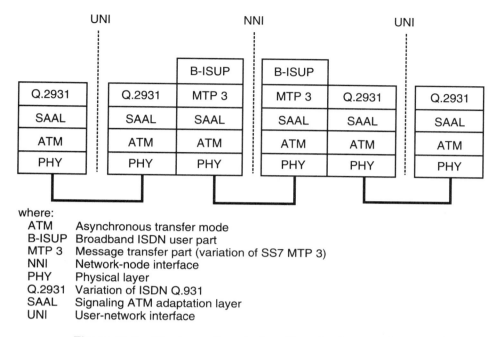

where:
ATM   Asynchronous transfer mode
B-ISUP   Broadband ISDN user part
MTP 3   Message transfer part (variation of SS7 MTP 3)
NNI   Network-node interface
PHY   Physical layer
Q.2931   Variation of ISDN Q.931
SAAL   Signaling ATM adaptation layer
UNI   User-network interface

Figure 6–1   The broadband signaling stacks and SAAL.

For the UNI, Q.2931 (a variation of ISDN's layer 3 Q.931) is used to set up
and tear down a connection. It operates over an AAL designed especially
for Q.2931, which is called the signaling AAL (SAAL). These layers operate over the conventional ATM layer and a selected physical layer.

For the NNI, the broadband ISUP (B-ISDN) and message transfer
part 3 (MTP 3) are variations of their counterparts in the SS7 signaling
standard. They rely on the SAAL to support their operations. These layers also operate over the conventional ATM and a selected physical layer.

The UNI and NNI SAALs have some similarities and differences.
Both contain a common part convergence sublayer (CPCS) and a segmentation and reassembly sublayer (SAR). However, in actual implementations, the NNI SAAL is likely to be more complex than the UNI SAAL
and performs a wide array of support services for B-ISUP and MTP 3.
These services are described later in this chapter.

The Protocol Stack in More Detail

Figure 6–2 is yet another level of detail and shows the protocol stack
for the signaling part of the NNI. The CES notations identify connection
endpoints (with connection endpoint suffixes) that are used in conjunc-

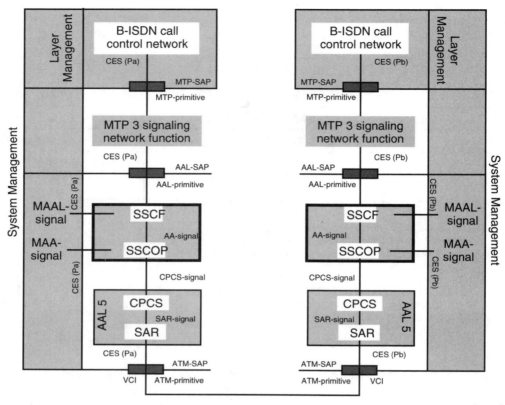

where:
CES   Connection end points
CPCS   Common part convergence sublayer
SAR   Segmentation and reassembly sublayer

Figure 6–2   Signaling stack for the NNI.

tion with service access points (SAPs) to identify a connection. SAPs are explained in Chapter 5. A one-to-one relationship exists between a connection endpoint within the AAL-SAP and a connection endpoint within the ATM-SAP. The communications between the entities in each exchange occur through the primitive and signaling operations, also described in Chapter 5. Remember, signals are used between layer entities that have no SAPs defined between them.

The layers above the ATM AAL (SSCF and SSCOP) are B-ISDN call control and MTP 3. B-ISDN call control is responsible for connection management, and MTP 3 is responsible for routing traffic between NNI nodes.

FUNCTIONS OF SAAL

The overall functions of the SAAL can be summarized as follows. SAAL is responsible for the correct transfer of data on a point-to-point ATM connection. One of its primary functions is to relieve the user (the upper layers in the signaling stack, B-ISUP and MTP 3) from any concern for data errors, loss, duplications, or insertions that may occur on the signaling link. SAAL restricts the length of user data from 5 to a maximum of 4096 octets.

SAAL provides a link monitoring service, that is similar to MTP 2 in a narrowband signaling stack. It "proves" that links are stable and error-free enough to be used (with alignment procedures). It can also take a link out of service when it becomes unreliable.

SAAL also provides for flow control procedures and employs mechanisms to insure that two exchanges do not create congestion problems with each other.

The sublayers of SAAL contribute to these overall functions. Let us take a brief look at them as a prelude to more detailed discussions.

Functions of SSCF

SSCF acts as a go-between for MTP 3 and SSCOP. As such, it maps primitives from MTP 3 to the required SSCOP signals and vice versa. In essence, it passes signals back and forth between SSCOP and MTP 3. As such, it does not send much information (PDUs) to its peer entity in the receiving exchange, but relies on SSCOP to convey its information in the SSCOP PDUs. Notwithstanding, it has other responsibilities as well. They are summarized here:

Flow Control: SSCF notifies the user about levels of congestion (or if no congestion exists) in order to prevent cell loss. It also regulates its flow of PDUs to the lower layers to prevent congestion at the other end.

Link Status: Based on primitives it receives from MTP 3 and SCCOP, SSCF maintains information (local state variables) about the status of the link, such as "aligned ready," "out of service," and so on. Using this information, it may generate primitives/signals to MTP 3 and SSCOP to aid in managing the link.

Layer Management: SSCF reports to layer management when a link is released. It relies upon layer management to help it in error monitoring functions.

Alignment Procedures: SSCF maintains the information (state variables) about all the alignment procedures that are taking place when a link is brought into service or taken out of service. These procedures are summarized below.

Alignment Procedures. A link is brought into service by a request from the user. The user is the upper layer resting above SSCF, typically MTP 3. At the request of the user (through the issuance of a request primitive), SSCF sends a PDU to its peer entity in the receiving exchange to start the process and moves from the "out of service" state to the "alignment" state for this link.

These operations require SSCOP to set up the link between two exchanges. When the link setup is finished, SSCF so indicates to layer management, which initiates error monitoring operations. SSCF then enters into the "proving" state for this link.

At this time, proving PDUs are transferred between the two exchanges. If the proving operation occurs successfully (transferring a specific number of PDUs across the link within a set time), SSCF instructs layer management to terminate the proving operations and sends a PDU to its peer to indicate that proving was successful. When it sends this PDU, SSCF enters into the "aligned-ready" state and upon receiving a confirmation of this PDU, it enters into the "in service" state.

A link is proved by the successful transfer of n number of proving PDUs during time period T3 (which is controlled by a timer). After T3 expires, if C_n number of proving PDUs have been sent successfully with no indications of problems, the link is considered aligned and placed into service.

Like MTP 2, SSCF alignment procedures provide for normal or emergency proving. With normal proving, a link must prove itself (determine it is reliable) for a set proving period before it is allowed to transmit live signals. Emergency proving is invoked from either MTP 3 or layer management. If it is invoked from MTP 3, proving is performed. If it is invoked from layer management, it means that layer management requests no proving.

Proving Algorithm. The ITU-T Q.2144 Recommendation defines the proving algorithm. Bellcore GR-2878-CORE provides an overview of the operation, which I have included here. The proving algorithm for SAAL links is based on of the alignment error rate monitor used for proving 56/64 kbit/s CCS links. Test PDUs are sent over the link at a specified rate r over a proving period of 1 minute. If the link suffers from one or more errors during this time, the proving is tried again. If no errors occur, the link is returned to service. The test PDU sending rate r is determined such that the proving procedure is in consonant with the in-service error monitor.

According to ITU-T Q.2144, if the existing error rate is such that the error monitor will take the link out of service in a matter of eight minutes or less, the proving algorithm should have almost zero probability of proving the link in 8 minutes (the craft alerting timer). The parameter r depends on the link speed, as specified in Section 9.4 of draft recommendation Q.2144. For a 1.5 Mbit/s link, $r = 1322$ cells/second, which corresponds to 0.365 Erlang load.

The SSCF PDU.   SSCF entities exchange only one PDU. It contains information on the status of the sending SSCF and is coded to indicate one of the following states or to indicate a problem: (1) out of service, (2) processor outage, (3) in service, (4) normal, (5) emergency, (6) alignment not successful, (7) management initiated, (8) protocol error, and (9) proving not successful.

Functions of SSCOP

One might wonder why another lower layer protocol is needed to support a signaling network. After all, earlier signaling networks performed well enough with MTP 2 at one of the lower layers (layer two) to support the upper layer signaling protocols (such as ISUP). The answer is that MTP 2, while well-designed and powerful in its functions, contains some operations and fields that are not needed in an ATM-based broadband signaling system. In retrospect, MTP 2 has also been found to be deficient in how it handles certain sequencing, flow control, and acknowledgments operations on the signaling link. Therefore, the standards groups decided that a new protocol was needed.

Like MTP 2, SSCOP keeps all signaling units (messages) that flow across the link in sequential order, and it also provides for retransmission of erred traffic. To make certain the communicating nodes (exchanges) are operational, each node executes a "keep alive" procedure with its neighbor node. SSCOP also contains a procedure that allows the local user to look at the SSCOP queue for purposes of determining the status of messages. The SSCOP also provides a number of status reporting operations.

SSCOP and AAL5.   Figure 6–3 shows the relationship of the SSCOP service data unit (SDU), the AAL5 CPCS service data unit, and the ATM cell. Beginning at the top part of the figure, the B-ISUP message is encap-

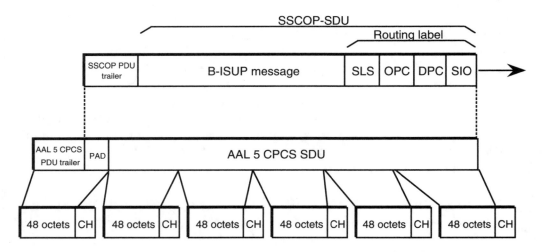

**Figure 6–3   SSCOP SDU, AAL 5 SDU, and the ATM cells.
(See footnote 1)**

sulated into the MTP 3 header (shown in this figure as the routing label). Then, the SSCOP trailer is placed behind these fields and sent to AAL5.[1] AAL5 adds its trailer and any PAD characters to ensure an even 48-byte (octet) boundary alignment. Traffic is then passed to segmentation operations and then to the ATM layer (depicted at the bottom part of this figure) where it is segmented into 48-byte traffic. Each 48-byte payload is appended with a cell header. This process is reversed at the receiver in accordance with conventional OSI depcapsulation operations.

Functions of SSCS Layer Management (LM)

The SSCS LM is the service specific convergence sublayer layer management entity. It interacts with the layers directly to perform a variety of operations, administration, and maintenance (OAM) functions. Thus, it is depicted as an entity that interacts with all the SAAL layers, except for CPCS and SAR (AAL type 5) where no interactions are defined. SSCS LM is tasked with the following responsibilities.

---

[1]Figure 6–3 shows the SSCOP PDU placed behind the B-ISUP, which I derived from the ANSI specifications. In practice, most systems place a L_2 header (SSCOP) in front of the MTP 3 routing label since the L_2 header is examined at the receiver before the routing label and the B-ISUP message. However, the figure is correct, and SSCOP is actually a logical L_2 protocol. The traditional L_2 functions of "frame delineation" with flags/preambles are performed by a layer operating below the ATM layer. (For example, a media access control [MAC] layer or the SONET physical layer.)

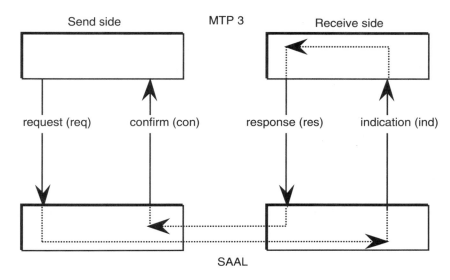

Figure 6–4   Primitives' relationships to the layers (MTP 3 and SAAL used in this example).

Layer management determines if a signaling link should be taken out of service or put into service (the latter function is called link proving). As part of these operations, links are monitored for excessive delays in the delivery of traffic. Layer management also permits a certain number of errors to occur on the link in order to avoid unnecessary changeovers to alternate links.

A number of ongoing measurements are taken by layer management. As examples, counters are maintained on how long each link has been in service, how often it has failed, how often and how many times the link has experienced congestion, and other information.

THE SAAL PRIMITIVES AND SIGNALS OPERATIONS

SAAL (and the ATM architecture in general) is organized around the OSI Model. As such, the layers in each ATM node interact with each other through primitives or signals.[2] Figure 6–4 shows how the primitives operate (MTP 3 and SAAL are used as the examples). Four transac-

---

[2]As a reminder, the term signal is used in place of a primitive if there is no service access point (SAP) defined between the user and provider (between the SAAL entities).

tions (primitives) are invoked to and from a layer through service access points (SAPs). (Primitives are explained in Chapter 5.) While the OSI Model defines four primitives, not all of them need be invoked to carry out an operation. Later discussions will explain how each of them is used by the SAAL sublayers.

Depictions of the Layers and Their Associated Primitives and Signals

Due to the variety of interfaces that exist between the SAAL sublayer entities, several sets of primitives and signals are defined, one for each interface. An understanding of these operations is fundamental to understanding the architecture of SAAL. To that end, Figure 6–5 shows all the primitives/signals and at which interface they operate. This figure will be a helpful reference tool for the material in this section of the chapter.

Two sets of primitives are not shown in Figure 6–5 and are explained in subsequent chapters. The primitives between Q.2931 and SAAL are described in Chapter 7. The primitives between MTP 3 and B-ISUP are explained in Chapter 8.

Primitives and Signals between SSCF and MTP 3

Table 6–1 lists the primitives that operate between SSCF and MTP 3 as well as the parameters that are passed with the primitives. The parameter labeled FSNC is the forward sequence number of the last message signal unit that was accepted by the remote peer entity. The parameter labeled BSNT is the backward sequence number that is transmitted to the remote peer entity. The congestion parameter is explained in Note 3 in Table 6–1. The message unit (mu) parameter contains the traffic passed between SSCF and MTP 3.

Many of the primitives are self-descriptive, but I will provide a summary of their use. Data are sent between MTP 3 and SSCF through the AAL-MESSAGE_FOR_TRANSMISSION and the AAL-RECEIVED_MESSAGE primitives. The former primitive is used by the AAL user to send data to SSCF, and the latter is used by AAL to deliver data to SSCF.

If the signaling link becomes congested, SSCF can notify the user with the AAL-LINK_CONGESTED primitive. Conversely, when the link is no longer congested, SSCF informs the user with the AAL-LINK_CONGESTION_CEASED primitive. (This latter primitive is not used in North America.) In addition, the congestion parameter in the AAL-LINK_CONGESTION primitive must indicate one of four levels of congestion numbered zero through three with zero meaning no congestion.

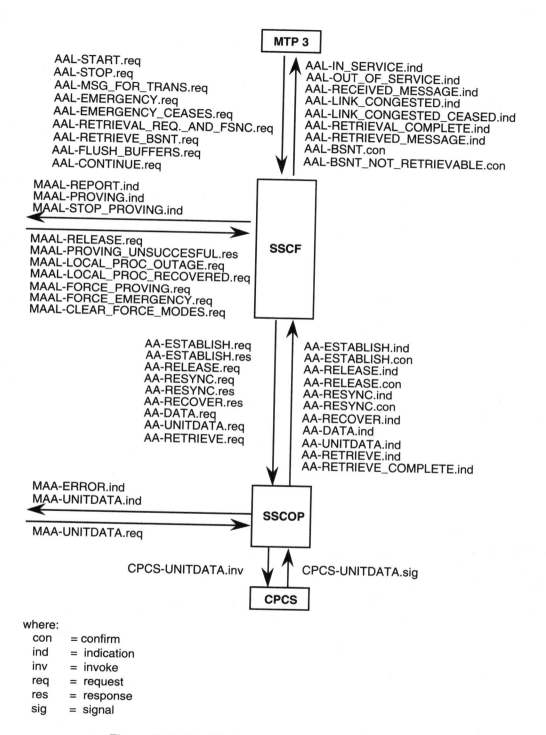

MTP 3

AAL-START.req
AAL-STOP.req
AAL-MSG_FOR_TRANS.req
AAL-EMERGENCY.req
AAL-EMERGENCY_CEASES.req
AAL-RETRIEVAL_REQ._AND_FSNC.req
AAL-RETRIEVE_BSNT.req
AAL-FLUSH_BUFFERS.req
AAL-CONTINUE.req

AAL-IN_SERVICE.ind
AAL-OUT_OF_SERVICE.ind
AAL-RECEIVED_MESSAGE.ind
AAL-LINK_CONGESTED.ind
AAL-LINK_CONGESTED_CEASED.ind
AAL-RETRIEVAL_COMPLETE.ind
AAL-RETRIEVED_MESSAGE.ind
AAL-BSNT.con
AAL-BSNT_NOT_RETRIEVABLE.con

MAAL-REPORT.ind
MAAL-PROVING.ind
MAAL-STOP_PROVING.ind

MAAL-RELEASE.req
MAAL-PROVING_UNSUCCESFUL.res
MAAL-LOCAL_PROC_OUTAGE.req
MAAL-LOCAL_PROC_RECOVERED.req
MAAL-FORCE_PROVING.req
MAAL-FORCE_EMERGENCY.req
MAAL-CLEAR_FORCE_MODES.req

SSCF

AA-ESTABLISH.req
AA-ESTABLISH.res
AA-RELEASE.req
AA-RESYNC.req
AA-RESYNC.res
AA-RECOVER.res
AA-DATA.req
AA-UNITDATA.req
AA-RETRIEVE.req

AA-ESTABLISH.ind
AA-ESTABLISH.con
AA-RELEASE.ind
AA-RELEASE.con
AA-RESYNC.ind
AA-RESYNC.con
AA-RECOVER.ind
AA-DATA.ind
AA-UNITDATA.ind
AA-RETRIEVE.ind
AA-RETRIEVE_COMPLETE.ind

MAA-ERROR.ind
MAA-UNITDATA.ind

MAA-UNITDATA.req

SSCOP

CPCS-UNITDATA.inv   CPCS-UNITDATA.sig

CPCS

where:
con   = confirm
ind   = indication
inv   = invoke
req   = request
res   = response
sig   = signal

Figure 6–5 The SAAL NNI interface architecture.

73

Table 6–1   Primitives between SSCF and MTP 3

	Primitive Type				Parameters in Primitive			
	res	ind	res	con	Message Unit	FSNC	BSNT	Congestion Parameter
AAL-MESSAGE_FOR TRANSMISSION	X				X			
AAL-RECEIVED_MESSAGE		X			X			
AAL-LINK_CONGESTED		X						X[1]
AAL-LINK_CONGESTION_CEASED[2]		X						
AAL-EMERGENCY	X							
AAL-EMERGENCY_CEASES	X							
AAL-STOP	X							
AAL-START	X							
AAL-IN_SERVICE		X						
AAL-OUT_OF_SERVICE		X						
AAL-RETRIEVE_BSNT	X							
AAL-RETRIEVAL_REQUEST_AND_FSNC	X					X		
AAL-RETRIEVED_MESSAGES		X			X			
AAL-RETRIEVAL_COMPLETE		X						
AAL-BSNT				X			X	
AAL-FLUSH_BUFFERS[3]	X							
AAL-CONTINUE[3]	X							
AAL-BSNT_NOT_RETRIEVABLE				X				

Notes:
1. In North American networks, the AAL-LINK_CONGESTED primitive must indicate one of four levels of congestion in the congestion parameter, levels 0 through 3, with 0 meaning no congestion.
2. The AAL-LINK_CONGESTION_CEASED primitive is not used in North American networks.
3. If these primitives occur they must be ignored (i.e., not implemented in ANSI specifications).

where:
  BSNT = Backward sequence number
  FSNC = Forward sequence number

MTP 3 can curtail link proving by sending the AAL-EMERGENCY primitive to SSCF, and it can request that SSCF return to its normal link proving operations by sending to SSCF the AAL-EMERGENCY_CEASES primitive.

To establish communications with another exchange, MTP 3 issues the AAL-START primitive, and when it wishes to inhibit further communications with the exchange, it sends the AAL-STOP primitive.

SSCF can inform MTP 3 about the status of a signaling link. It uses the AAL-IN_SERVICE primitive to inform MTP 3 that a link is available and the AAL-OUT_OF_SERVICE to indicate a link is not available.

In the ANSI specifications, AAL-FLUSH_BUFFERS and AAL-CONTINUE primitives are not implemented.

For ongoing management of the link, MTP 3 and SSCF have access to several primitives to request and inform each other about a number of operations. MTP 3 invokes the AAL-RETRIEVE_BSNT primitive to request the BSNT value to be retrieved and SSCF responds with the AAL-BSNT.confirm. If the BSNT value is not available, SSCF will send MTP 3 the AAL-BSNT_NOT_RETRIEVABLE.

Finally, MTP 3 can request nonacknowledged messages to be delivered by presenting the AAL-RETRIEVAL_REQUEST_AND_FSNC primitive to SSCF. In turn, SSCF delivers nonacknowledged messages to MTP 3 with two primitives: AAL-RETRIEVED_MESSAGES and AAL-RETRIEVAL_COMPLETE.

Table 6–2   Signals between SSCF and SSCOP and SSCOP and Layer Management

	Type and Associated Parameters			
Signal	*Request*	*Indication*	*Response*	*Confirm*
AA-ESTABLISH	SSCOP-UU, BR	SSCOP-UU	SSCOP-UU, BR	SSCOP-UU
AA-RELEASE	SSCOP-UU	SSCOP-UU Source	Not defined	—
AA-DATA	MU	MUSN	Not defined	Not defined
AA-RESYNC	SSCOP-UU	SSCOP-UU	—	—
AA-RECOVER	Not defined	—	—	Not defined
AA-UNITDATA	MU	MU	Not defined	Not defined
AA-RETRIEVE	RN	MU	Not defined	Not defined
AA-RETRIEVE COMPLETE	Not defined	—	Not defined	Not defined
MAA-ERROR	Not defined	Code, Count	Not defined	Not defined
MAA-UNITDATA	MU	MU	Not defined	Not defined

—: The signal has no parameters
Note: The SSCF PDU can be placed in the MU parameter of AA-DATA.req or in the SSCOP-UU of the AA-ESTABLISH.req or AA-RELEASE.req
where:
BR   Buffer release
MU   Message unit
MUSN   Message unit sequence number
RN   Retrieval number
UU   User-to-user

Signals between SSCOP-SSCF and SSCOP-Layer Management

Table 6–2 lists the signals that are exchanged between SSCOP and SSCF and SSCOP and layer management. The specific operations pertaining to the signals are explained next, and several examples of the use of these signals and parameters are provided in the next section of this chapter.

In order to establish connections between two exchanges and release these connections, SSCF and SSCOP exchange the AA-ESTABLISH and AA-RELEASE signals respectively. The AA-RESYNC signals are used to resynchronize the SSCOP connection and the AA-RECOVER signals are used to recover from an error occurring during an ongoing operation.

The AA-DATA signals are used for assured transfer of data between the exchanges.

In contrast, the AA-UNITDATA signals are used for nonassured transfer of data between layer management and SSCOP. The AA-UNIT-DATA signal also supports broadcast operations between multiple exchanges. The other signal exchanged between layer management and SSCOP is the MAA-ERROR signal. It is used to indicate the type of protocol error that has occurred. The reader should refer to Annex A of ANSI T1.637-1994 for information on these error conditions. As a general statement, they cover problems dealing with timer expirations, receiving erroneous PDUs, unsuccessful retransmissions, and others.

The AA-RETRIEVE and AA-RETRIEVE_COMPLETE signals are used to exchange data from SSCOP to SSCF.

Parameters in the Signals. The parameters that are associated with these signals are also listed in Table 6–2. They have the following functions.

The message unit (MU) parameter contains user information. For the request signals, the parameter is mapped directly into the information field of the SSCOP PDU. For the indication signals, this field is derived from the contents of the information field of an incoming SSCOP PDU. The one exception to these comments pertains to the AA-RETRIEVE.indication signals, in which case the MU parameter contains a message that is returned to the SSCOP user from a queue containing data awaiting transmission.

The SSCOP user-to-user (SSCOP-UU) parameter contains end user traffic. The parameter correlates directly with the SSCOP-UU field in the SSCOP PDU.

The message unit sequence number (MUSN) parameter is derived from the N(S) field of the incoming SD PDU.

The retrieval number (RN) parameter, as its name implies, is used to retrieve data. It is sent by SSCF to request that SSCOP retrieve data from the transmission buffer. It can be coded to obtain the following services:

- Identification of the first SD PDU to be retrieved
- Retrieval of only those SD PDUs that have not yet been transmitted
- Indication that all SD PDUs are to be retrieved

The buffer release (BR) parameter is used during the connection setup to indicate if the transmitting SSCOP is allowed to release its buffers when the connection is released. It can be coded also to allow the release of selectively acknowledged messages from the transmission buffer.

The code parameter is an error code that indicates what type of problem has occurred during an ongoing operation, (Table 6–5).

The source parameter indicates to the SSCOP user whether the local or remote exchange originated a connection release.

And, finally, the count parameter indicates the number of SD PDUs that have been retransmitted.

Signals between Layer Management and SSCF

Table 6–3 lists the signals that are exchanged between layer management and SSCF. This section provides a summary of the functions of these signals. The MAAL-PROVING. ind is sent by SSCF to initiate error monitoring by layer management; it is part of the link proving process. If the proving is not successful, layer management sends the MAAL-PROVING_UNSUCCESSFUL.res to SSCF. If proving is to be terminated, SSCF sends the MAAL-STOP_PROVING.ind to layer management.

Layer management (LM) can also initiate forced proving by sending the MAAL-FORCE_PROVING.req to SSCF, and proving can be omitted by layer management sending SSCF the MAAL-FORCE_EMERGENCY.req signal. If layer management does not care which proving mode is used, it sends SSCF the MAAL-CLEAR_FORCE_MODES.req signal.

If a local processor fails or if a failed processor has been placed back into service, layer management sends to SSCF the MAAL-LOCAL_PROCESSOR_OUTAGE.req and MAAL-LOCAL_PROCESSOR_RECOVERED.req signals respectively.

Table 6–3 Signals Between Layer Management and SCCF.

Signals	Signal Type and Associated Parameters			
	Request	Indication	Response	Confirm
MAAL-PROVING		X		
MAAL-CLEAR_FORCE_MODES	X			
MAAL-FORCE_EMERGENCY	X			
MAAL-FORCE_PROVING	X			
MAAL-STOP_PROVING		X		
MAAL-PROVING_UNSUCCESSFUL			X	
MAAL-RELEASE	X			
MAAL-LOCAL_PROCESSOR_OUTAGE	X			
MAAL-LOCAL_PROCESSOR_RECOVERED	X			
MAAL-REPORT		X		

Note: For an explanation of the parameters in these signals, refer to "Parameters in the Signals"

SSCF can notify layer management about a variety of events with the MAAL-REPORT.ind signal. Its purpose is to give layer management a clear view of the status of SSCF. As examples, this signal can contain information (1) on the state of a SSCOP connection, (2) about whether the connection has been released or an indication of the origination of the release (local or remote), (3) about congestion, and (4) types of errors that have been encountered on the link.

Finally, layer management can instruct SSCF to release a connection by sending it the MAAL-RELEASE.req signal.

Parameters in the Signals. The large number of parameters in the signals precludes a detailed discussion (many of them deal with the state transitions of SSCF, which is described in an 11-page table [Table 6] in ANSI T1.645-1995). As a general description, the parameters describe the state of an SSCOP connection (in service alignment not successful, etc.) and the reasons for the transitions from one state to another.

SIGNALS BETWEEN SSCOP AND CPCS

Two signals are passed between SSCOP and CPCS, (Table 6–4). The CPCS-UNITDATA.invoke is used by SSCOP to send SSCOP PDUs to its peer, by placing the PDU in the interface data (ID) parameter of CPCS-

Table 6–4   Signals between SSCOP and CPCS

Name	Parameters
CPCS-UNITDATA.invoke	ID, LP, CI, CPCS-UU
CPCS-UNITDATA.signal	ID, LP, CI, CPCS-UU

Note: Only ID is used at this time. The terms LP, CI, UU are not explained in either the ANSI or ITU-T specifications. I have notified these organizations of this omission.

ID	Interface data
LP	Ignored or not defined
CI	Ignored or not defined
UU	Ignored or not defined

UNITDATA.invoke. Conversely, the CPCS-UNITDATA.signal is used to receive messages from the peer; the SSCOP PDUs also reside in the ID parameter. The other parameters in the signals are ignored or not defined.

THE ERROR CODES

As explained in the previous section, a code parameter is used to indicate the type of problem that has occurred during an SSCOP operation. Table 6–5 shows the error codes that SSCOP may pass to layer management via the MAA-ERROR.ind signal. (The right-most column is explained in the next section of this chapter.)

THE SSCOP OPERATIONS IN MORE DETAIL

Before we analyze SSCOP operations, it will be helpful to briefly digress to explain the rationale for some of SSCOP's behavior. First, you will notice that SSCOP performs many conventional layer two functions, such as the sequencing and acknowledgment of traffic. Second, SSCOP employs a rather elaborate sequencing and acknowledgment scheme to do its job, in comparison to other protocols that perform similar services, such as MTP 2, LAPD, or LAPB.

The reason for these measures is that SSCOP is more efficient than its predecessors in managing the link. This link efficiency translates into a more "elaborate" protocol, but as we shall see, it is well-designed and elegantly simple.

Before the SCCOP operations are demonstrated, it is necessary to examine the SSCOP PDUs (messages).

Table 6–5   Error Codes in the code parameter

Type of Error	Code	PDU or Other Event That Creates Error Condition
Receipt of unsolicited or inappropriate PDU	A	SD PDU
	B	BGN PDU
	C	BGAK PDU
	D	BGREJ PDU
	E	END PDU
	F	ENDAK PDU
	G	POLL PDU
	H	STAT PDU
	I	USTAT PDU
	J	RS
	K	RSAK PDU
	L	ER
	M	ERAK
Unsuccessful retransmission	O	VT(CC) >= MaxCC
	P	Timer_NO-RESPONSE expiry
Other list elements error type	Q	SD or POLL, N(S) error
	R	STAT N(PS) error
	S	STAT N(R) or list elements error
	T	USTAT N(R) or list elements error
	U	PDU length violation
SD loss	V	SD PDUs must be retransmitted
Credit condition	W	Lack of credit
	X	Credit obtained

SSCOP PDUs

Table 6–6 lists the SSCOP PDUs that are exchanged between SSCOP peer-entities in two different ATM signaling nodes. The function of each PDU is shown as well as a brief description of the PDU's operations. Later material explains these PDUs in more detail with some examples. Table 6–6 is a summary of the following explanations of the PDUs.

- Begin (BGN): This PDU establishes a connection between two peer SSCOP entities. It is a housekeeping function in that it clears buffers and initializes transmit and receive counters.
- Begin acknowledge (BGAK): This PDU acknowledges the connection request; that is, the BGN PDU.

- Begin reject (BGREJ): This PDU rejects the connection request; once again, the BGN PDU.
- End (END): This PDU releases the connection between the two communicating parties.
- End acknowledge (ENDAK): This PDU confirms the release; that is, the END PDU.
- Resynchronization (RS): This PDU acts as a conventional connection-oriented reset found in other connection-oriented protocols. It resynchronizes the buffers as well as the transmitter and receiver state variables (counters).
- Resynchronization acknowledge (RSAK): This PDU acknowledges the resynchronization request by the peer entity; that is, the RS PDU.
- Error recovery (ER): This PDU recovers from errors occurring during the connection operations.

Table 6–6   Summary of the SSCOP Protocol Data Units (PDUs)

Function	PDU Name	Description
Establishment	BGN	Request initialization
	BGAK	Request acknowledgment
	BGREJ	Connection reject
Release	END	Disconnect command
	ENDAK	Disconnect acknowledgment
Resynchronization	RS	Resynchronization command
	RSAK	Resynchronization acknowledgment
Recovery	ER	Recovery command
	ERAK	Recovery acknowledgment
Assured data transfer	SD	Sequenced connection-mode data
	POLL	Transmitter state information with request for receive state information
	STAT	Solicited receiver state information
	USTAT	Unsolicited receiver state information
Unacknowledged data transfer	UD	Unnumbered user data
Management data transfer	MD	Unnumbered management data

- Error recovery acknowledge (ERAK): This PDU acknowledges the recovery request; that is, the ER PDU.
- Sequenced data (SD): This PDU transfers user traffic (traffic from the upper layers) to the peer entity.
- Status request (POLL): This PDU requests status information about the operations at the peer SSCOP entity.
- Solicited status response (STAT): This PDU responds to the POLL PDU. It is used to inform the polling entity about the correct reception of traffic (SD PDUs). It is also used for window control and contains a credit value to provide guidance to the poller about how much more traffic it can or cannot send. This PDU also contains the sequence number that was transmitted in the POLL PDU (N(PS)).
- Unsolicited status response (USTAT): This PDU is transmitted to the peer entity when missing SDUs are detected, which is based on comparing the sequence numbers of the incoming SD PDUs. This PDU also contains the credit field for window control.
- Unnumbered data (UD): This PDU is used to transmit unsequenced traffic between the SSCOP users. It does not affect the ongoing connection-oriented sequencing nor does it alter any counters or states between the two entities. This type of traffic may be discarded or lost without either party being notified of the event.
- Management data (MD): This PDU transmits non-sequenced management information between two SSCOP management entities. It carries the same risks (regarding possible loss) as the UD PDU.

It is also important to explain the parameters (fields) that are carried in the PDUs. You should refer to this section in conjunction with the operations that are described next.

- N(SQ): This field is a connection sequence value. It is carried in a BGN, RS, or ER PDU. It is used with a counter at the receiver to identify any retransmissions of these three types of PDUs.
- N(S): This is a send sequence number that is placed in each newly transmitted SD or POLL PDU.
- N(PS): This field is carried in a POLL PDU at the transmitting site. The receiver of the POLL maps this field into a returned STAT PDU. In this manner, each POLL and its associated STAT can be correlated with each other.

- *N(R):* This field is carried in a STAT or USTAT PDU. It is a receive sequence number and is used to acknowledge transmissions.
- *N(MR):* This field is carried in the following PDUs: STAT, USTAT, RS, RSAK, ER, ERAK, BGN, BGAK. It is used to indicate if the peer SSCOP entity can send (a grant credit) or not send more traffic.

Examples of SSCOP "Housekeeping" Operations

This section should tie together many of the concepts that have been explained thus far in this chapter. Several examples are shown shortly, and the reader is encouraged to study Annexes D and E of ANSI T1.637 for more detailed explanations.

We have examined several aspects of SAAL and discussed briefly about the relationships between primitives and PDUs. Let us now see how they are used together.

An Example of the Relationship of SSCF/SSCOP Primitives and the SSCOP PDUs. As shown in Figure 6–6, to set up a connection between two SAAL entities, SSCF issues an AA-ESTABLISH.req primitive to SSCOP. This primitive contains the SSCOP-UU and BR parameters, which are used by SSCOP to create the BGN message. This message is sent to the receiving SSCOP where it is decoded, acted upon, and mapped to the AA-ESTABLISH.ind primitive sent to the receiving SSCF. This SSCF responds with the AA-ESTABLISH.res primitive to its SSCOP, which also contains the SSCOP-UU and BR parameters. In turn, the SSCOP sends the BGAK message back to the originating SSCOP, which decodes it, acts upon it, and passes it to its SSCF. These actions set up the connections at the two SAAL entities in the two broadband signaling exchanges.

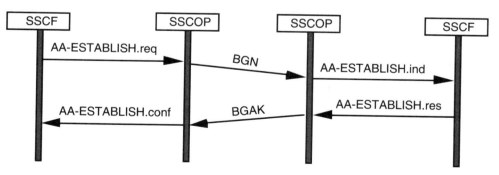

Figure 6–6   Example of SSCF and SSCOP operations.

Other housekeeping operations are part of SAAL and SSCOP activities, and follow similar procedures shown in the time sequence diagram in Figure 6–6, but one time sequence diagram should suffice.

Examples of SSCOP Transferring Signaling Traffic

As examples of how some of the PDU fields are used, ANSI provides a useful table in ANSI T1.637-1994 Annex D. The reader should use Table 6–7 as a reference as you study this section. Generally speaking, the purpose of the acknowledgments is to selectively reject, and/or accept the received PDUs. The "x" in the table means the PDU was not received correctly, or not received. The numbers between the { } are list elements and inform the receiver of the message which PDUs are acceptable, and which PDUs must be resent.

Figure 6–7 provides a general example of SSCOP operations in which no errors occur. A poll timer (called the TIMER_POLL in the specifications) is used to control the sending of periodic polls. Another timer (NO-RESPONSE) is used in parallel with the poll timer. During its interval, at least one STAT PDU must be received or the connection is aborted. The POLL PDU invokes the STAT PDU; the purpose of the STAT PDU is to find out about the status of the sequenced data units it had previously sent to its peer SSCOP entity (SCCOP B).

Next, the receiving of the AA-DATA.req signal from SSCF A directs SCCOP A to send an SD PDU. Recall from Table 6–2 that this signal contains the message unit (MU), which is traffic from MTP 3 and B-ISUP, and the MU sequence number (MUSN). Thus, SSCF is responsible for the sequencing operations on the signaling link.

Table 6–7   The SSCOP List

Received PDUs	Received POLL PDU	Responding PDU[1]
1,x,x,4	For USTAT	USTAT(N(R)=2{2,4})
1,x,x,4	POLL(N(S)=5)	STAT(N(R)=2{2,4,5})
1,x,x,x	POLL(N(S)=5)	STAT(N(R)=2,{2,5})
1x,x,4,5	POLL(N(S)=6)	STAT(N(R)=2{2,4,6})
1,x,x,4,5,x,x	POLL(N(S)=8)	STAT(N(R)=2,{2,4,6,8})
1,x,x,4,5,x,x,8,9	POLL(N(S)=10)	STAT(N(R)=2,{2,4,6,8,10})

[1]Odd elements in the list indicate first PDU of a missing gap. Even elements indicate first PDU of a received sequence, except possibly the last one.

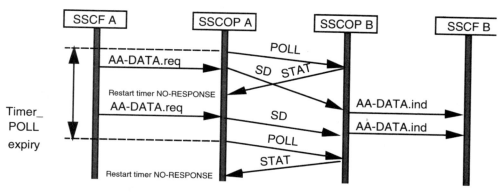

Figure 6–7   Data transfer with polls.

The initial POLL operation from SSCOP A begat the STAT PDU from SCCOP B. Upon receiving this PDU, SSCOP A restarts the NO-RESPONSE timer (which is restarted each time a STAT PDU is received). The issuance of POLL PDUs at SSCOP A is controlled by the POLL timer.

Figure 6–7 shows SSCOP operating in its active phase. It operates in the active phase as long as an SD or an ACK is outstanding. If the TIMER_POLL expires and there are no SDs or ACKs outstanding, but a STAT PDU is still outstanding, SSCOP enters into the transit phase.

Upon entering the transit phase, SSCOP starts the KEEP_ACTIVE timer (and continues to use the NO-RESPONSE timer). Upon receiving the STAT PDU, SSCOP stops the KEEP_ACTIVE and NO_RESPONSE timers, starts the IDLE timer and enters into the idle phase. During this phase SSCOP sends no polls and sends/receives no SD PDUs. Upon either a poll or SD being sent or received, SSCOP once again enters the active phase.

There is not much more to be said about the operations in Figure 6–7 except that the SD PDU message units are delivered to SSCF B (and then to MTP 3 and B-ISUP) by the AA-DATA.ind signals.

Figure 6–8 shows an SSCOP operation in more detail, with the primitives between SSCF and SSCOP excluded. SD PDUs are sent, with each succeeding PDU having its $N(S)$ field incremented by one. The $N(R)$ field in the PDU is set to 0, because the SSCOP A is expecting the SSCOP B to send its first PDU, which would be numbered $N(S) = 0$ (assuming it would be the first PDU sent since initialization, or that operations had wrapped that counter around to 0 again).

The POLL PDU solicits a STAT PDU. The $N(S)$ field is also used in the POLL and is set to 3 in the POLL. The $N(PS)$ value must be the same

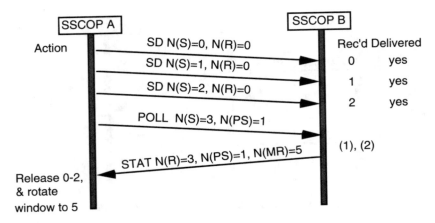

Notes:
1. Receiver of POLL maps *N(PS)* into field of STAT *N(PS)*
2. STAT *N(R)* = 3 is acknowledging SD PDUs, not the POLL.

Figure 6–8 Data transfer, with credit.

in the POLL and STAT, in order to correlate the two PDUs together.[3] The N(MR) = 5 is the credit value and rotates the send window to 5. So, SSCOP A can send PDUs up to 5, without waiting for a response.

At SSCOP B, the successful reception of SD PDUs 0, 1, and 2 allow SSCOP to deliver the message units to SSCF, noted by the "delivered" entries in Figure 6–8.

Figure 6–9 shows how SSCOP recovers from an error. SSCOP A sends four SD PDUs to SSCOP B, which are sequenced with $N(S) = 0$ through 3. All PDUs arrive at SSCOP correctly except PDU 1. SSCOP is not allowed to deliver out-of-sequence traffic to its user, so SSCOP B holds PDUs 2 and 3 in its buffer, and delivers PDU 0 to the user. It sends a USTAT PDU to SSCOP with $N(R) = 1$. This value informs SSCOP that PDU 1 should be retransmitted. (The $N(MR) = n$ is the credit value and not discussed in this example.)

The list element (LE) is set to 1,2, which conveys the following information. The odd element (the value of 1) specifies the PDU of a missing gap, which in this simple example is 1 (and the same value of the $N(R)$ value). The even element (the value of 2) specifies the first PDU of the next correctly received sequence. This information tells SSCOP A that:

---

[3]There is a conflict in the ANSI T1.637 document regarding the incrementing of $N(S)$ for the POLL PDU. Clause 7.4 a) (page 22) states that it is updated only for a SD PDU, but examples and clause 7.4 b) (page 23) contradict the former clause. I have notified ANSI, and this chapter assumes $N(S)$ is incremented for both PDUs.

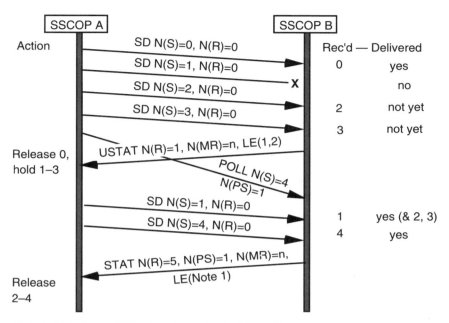

Note 1: List element (LE) is not needed in this PDU.

Figure 6–9   Recovery from an error.

(1) It must resend PDU 1; (2) it can release PDU 0 from its buffer; and (3) it must continue to hold PDUs 1, 2, and 3, because it does not yet have enough information about the fate of PDUs 2 and 3.

Before SSCOP A received the USTAT PDU from SSCOP B, it sent a POLL PDU. This message contains $N(S) = 4$, which represents the $N(S)$ value of the next new SD PDU (that is, an SD PDU that is to be transmitted for the first time). The POLL also contains $N(PS) = 1$. As discussed earlier, this is a sequence number of the POLL PDU. Upon receiving the USTAT PDU, SSCOP A resends SD 1, and sends SD 4 for the first time. These PDUs are received correctly by SSCOP B, which can now release PDUs 1, 2, 3, and 4 to the user. SSCOP B responds to the POLL PDU with the USTAT PDU which is coded with $N(R) = 5$ to inclusively acknowledge PDUs 1–4, and indicate it is expecting PDU 5 next. The $N(PS)$ field in the USTAT must be the same value as the $N(PS)$ field in the associated POLL PDU (a value of 1 in this example). As the note explains, no LEs need be coded in the PDU since there are not missing PDUs. The $N(R) = 4$ is sufficient to account for all traffic.

The final example (Figure 6–10) of SSCOP operations shows how the protocol recovers from multiple errors. SSCOP A sends eleven PDUs (with

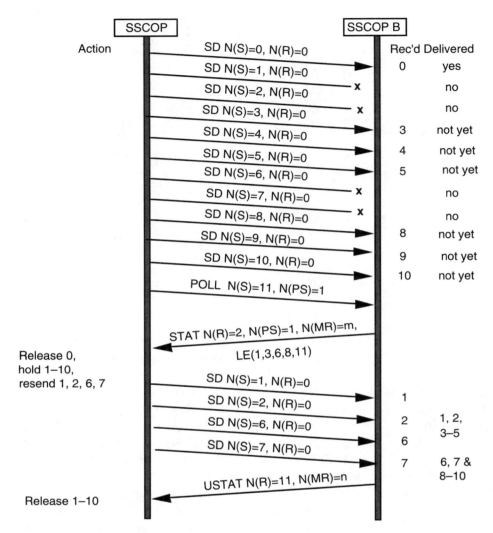

Figure 6–10   Recovery from multiple errors.

$N(S) = 0$ through 10) to SSCOP B. PDUs 1, 2, and 6, 7 are not received correctly and are not delivered to the SSCOP B user. The PDUs that are received correctly are either delivered to the user (PDU 1) if their delivery keeps them in sequential order, or are held to await the retransmissions of the erred PDUs. So, PDUs 3, 4, 5, and 8, 9, 10 are held by SSCOP B.

SSCOP A sends a POLL PDU to SSCOP B, with $N(S)$ set to 11. This value means that SSCOP has sent PDUs of 0–10 inclusive and intends to send PDU 11 next. The POLL PDU asks SSCOP to respond with a status message about which PDUs it has or has not received correctly.

SSCOP B responds with the STAT PDU. The list of elements (LEs) is coded to indicate the missing gaps. Remember the list is interpreted as: Odd elements identify the first PDU of a missing gap, and even elements identify the first PDU of a received sequence of PDUs, except possibly the last.

SSCOP A uses the information to resend PDUs 1, 2, 6, and 7, which are received correctly by SSCOP B. This entity responds with the USTAT PDU with the N(R) value set to 11, which inclusively acknowledges all the PDUs sent from SSCOP A.

RELATIONSHIPS OF THE SAAL ENTITIES AND MTP 3

Finally, Figure 6–11 shows one example of the relationships of the SAAL entities and MTP 3. This example is the initiation of a connection setup between two exchanges. MTP 3 at exchange A starts the process for sending an AAL-START.req primitive to SSCF A, which uses this information to form an AA-ESTABLISH.req primitive to send to SSCOP A. In turn, SSCOP A uses this information to create a BGN PDU to send to its peer SSCOP entity at exchange B. Notice that SSCF A returns the

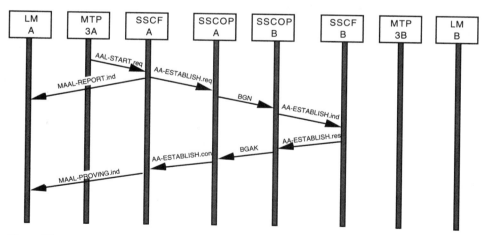

Note: The same set of procedures occur from exchange B (and MTP 3B), but are not shown in this figure.

Figure 6–11   Example of SAAL entity relationships.

MAAL-REPORT.ind signal to layer management A (LM A). Since link proving has just begun, this signal contains information that the link is not (yet) in service.

The BGN PDU parameters are used by SSCOP B to create an AA-ESTABLISH.ind primitive for transferal to SSCF B. No further information is sent to the entities at exchange B, but as the note in Figure 6–11 states, an identical operation is invoked at exchange B, but not shown in this example.

SSCF B examines the AA-ESTABLISH.req primitive and parameters, and responds with the AA-ESTABLISH.res primitive. This primitive is used by SSCOP B to create the BGAK PDU, which is sent to SSCOP A. The end result of this exchange is to notify LM A of the proving operations with the MAAL-PROVING.ind primitive.

Parameters in the Primitives and PDUs

Figure 6–12 shows the parameters that are associated with the primitives and PDUs. Their functions are as follows:

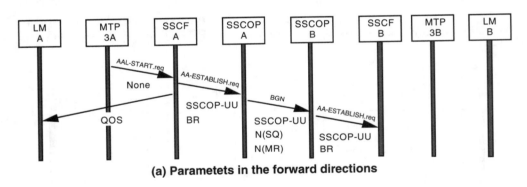

(a) Parametets in the forward directions

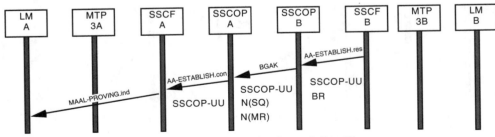

(b) Parameters in the backward direction

Figure 6–12   Parameters in the primitives.

- *SSCOP-UU*: This parameter is a user-to-user message. Its contents are application-dependent and may be null (not present).
- *BR*: This parameter is the buffer release. It indicates if the sender can release its buffers after the connection is released. It is also used during ongoing operations to release selectively acknowledged messages from the transmit buffer.
- *N(SQ)*: This parameter contains a connection sequence number. It is used to identify retransmitted BGN, RS, or ER PDUs.
- *N(MR)*: This parameter is used to set up the initial flow control operations (it is a window size parameter). The value establishes an initial credit between the SSCOPs to govern how many PDUs they can send to each other.
- *QOS* (quality of service): Optional features, that are tailored to a specific implementation.

SUMMARY

SAAL is responsible for the correct transfer of signaling data on a broadband signaling link. It relieves the user of concern about data errors, loss, duplicates, or insertions that may occur on the signaling link.

SAAL provides a link monitoring service, and "proves" that links are stable and error-free enough to be used (with alignment procedures). It can also take a link out of service if it becomes unreliable. SAAL also provides for flow control procedures and employs mechanisms to insure that two exchanges do not create congestion problems.

SSCF and SSCOP are the protocol entities that make up the SAAL operations, and these overall operations are coordinated by layer management (LM).

7

UNI Signaling

INTRODUCTION

This chapter examines the ATM signaling operations at the UNI. The operations deal with call and connection control procedures. Emphasis is placed on how connections are set up on demand between users and the ATM network. This procedure is also known as a switched virtual call (SVC) in older technology. The Q.2931 connection control protocol is explained, and the Q.2931 messages and their contents are analyzed.

This chapter is organized around the ITU-T Q.2931 Recommendation. The ATM Forum UNI Signaling Specification (version 4.0) is based on Q.2931, but has several variations of Q.2931. The major variations are also explained in this chapter.

BROADBAND SIGNALING STACKS

Figure 7–1 compares the ATM signaling stacks (protocol stacks) for UNI and NNI operations. For the UNI, Q.2931 (a variation of ISDN's layer 3 Q.931) is used to set up and tear down a connection. It operates over an AAL designed especially for Q.2931, which is called the signaling AAL (SAAL). I explain more about SAAL shortly. These layers operate over the conventional ATM layer and a selected physical layer.

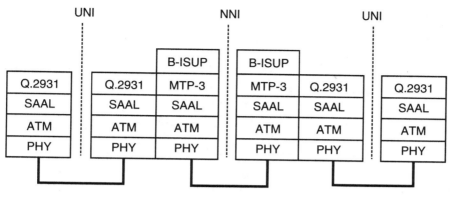

where:
ATM   Asynchronous transfer mode
B-ISUP   Broadband ISDN user part
MTP-3   Message transfer part (variation of SS7 MTP-3)
NNI   Network node interface
PHY   Physical layer
Q.2931 Variation of ISDN Q.931
SAAL   Signaling ATM adaptation layer
UNI   User network interface

Figure 7–1   Broadband signaling stacks.

For the NNI, the broadband ISDN (B-ISDN) and message transfer part 3 (MTP 3) are variations of their counterparts in the SS7 signaling standard. They rely on the SAAL to support their operations. These layers also operate over the conventional ATM and a selected physical layer.

The UNI and NNI SAALs have some similarities and differences. Both contain a common part convergence sublayer (CPCS) and a segmentation and reassembly sublayer (SAR). However, the NNI SAAL is more complex than the UNI SAAL, and performs wide array of support services for B-ISUP and MTP 3. These services are described later in this chapter.

UNI MESSAGES AND INFORMATION ELEMENTS

Signaling at the UNI requires that a wide variety of information be exchanged between the user and the network. This section provides a description of the messages and parameters that are used in these exchanges.

Message Format

Figure 7–2 shows the format of the Q.2931 message. The protocol discriminator field can be coded to identify the Q.2931 message, or other layer 3 protocols, such as ISDN Q.931, a frame relay SVC message in a frame relay network. Obviously, it is coded in this protocol to identify Q.2931 messages and is set to 00010001.

The call reference identifies each call and is assigned by the originating side of the call (the user at the local side, and the network at the remote side); therefore, it does not have end-to-end significance. Its purpose is to keep the different calls uniquely identified, and it remains fixed for the duration of the call. The call reference field contains a 1-bit call reference flag, which is used to identify which end of the signaling virtual channel originated the call reference. The origination side sets this bit to 0 and the destination side sets it to 1. Thus, this flag is used to avoid simultaneous attempts to allocate the same call reference value.

The message type identifies the specific type of message, such as a SETUP, ADD PARTY, and so on.

The information elements contain the fields that are used to control the connection operation. They contain information of the AAL and QOS operations that are to be supported during the connection.

				Bits				
8	7	6	5	4	3	2	1	Octets
Protocol discriminator								1
0	0	0	0	Length of call reference				2
Flag	Call reference value							3
Call reference value (continued)								4
Call reference value (continued)								5
Message type								6
Message type (continued)								7
Message length								8
Message length (continued)								9
Variable length information elements								n

Figure 7–2   Contents of the Q.2931 message.

The Messages

Table 7–1 lists the ATM messages and their functions employed for demand connections at the UNI. Since these messages are derived from Q.931, they contain the typical Q.931 fields such as protocol discriminator, call reference, message type, and message length. The information content of the field, of course, is tailored for the specific ATM UNI interface.

The Information Elements (IEs)

The functions of the information elements are summarized in Table 7–2. Many of the information elements are optional. It is the job of the ATM switch to map the contents of these information elements into operations at the NNI, and to map them back at the remote UNI.

OVERVIEW OF UNI OPERATIONS

As depicted in Figure 7–3, the connection establishment procedures begin by a user issuing the SETUP message. This message is sent by the calling user to the network and is relayed by the network to the called

Table 7–1   ATM Connection Control Messages

Message	Function
Call establishment	
SETUP	Initiate the call establishment
CALL PROCEEDING	Call establishment has begun
CONNECT	Call has been accepted
CONNECT ACKNOWLEDGE	Call acceptance has been acknowledged
Call clearing	
RELEASE	Initiate call clearing
RELEASE COMPLETE	Call has been cleared
Miscellaneous	
STATUS ENQUIRY (SE)	Sent to solicit a status message
STATUS (S)	Sent in response to SE or to report error
Global call reference	
RESTART	Restart all VCs
RESTART ACKNOWLEDGE	ACKS the RESTART
Point-to-multipoint operations	
ADD PARTY	Add party to an existing connection
ADD PARTY ACKNOWLEDGE	ACKS the ADD PARTY
ADD PARTY REJECT	REJECTS the ADD PARTY
DROP PARTY	Drops party from an existing connection
DROP PARTY ACKNOWLEDGE	ACKS the DROP PARTY

Table 7–2 Functions of the Information Service Elements

Element	Function
Protocol discriminator	Distinguishes different types of messages within ITU-T standards and standards bodies throughout the world
Call reference	Uniquely identifies each call at the UNI
Message type	Identifies type of message, such as SETUP, STATUS, etc.
Message length	Length of message excluding the three elements above and this element
AAL parameters	AAL parameters selected by user
ATM user cell rate	Specifies set of traffic parameters
Broadband bearer capability	Indicates several network bearer services (end-to-end timing, CBR, VBR, point-to-point, multipoint services)
Broadband high layer information	End-user codes, passed transparently through ATM network; identifies upper layer protocols or a vendor-specific application
Broadband repeat indicator	Used to allow repeated information elements to be interpreted correctly
Broadband low layer information	End-user codes, passed transparently through ATM network; identifies lower layer protocols/configurations
Called party number	Called party of the call
Called party subaddress	Called party subaddress
Calling party number	Origin party number
Calling party subaddress	Calling party subaddress
Call state	One of 12 values describing status of a call (active, call initiated, etc.)
Cause	Diagnostic codes
Connection identifier	The VPI and VCI for the call
QOS parameter	QOS class
Broadband sending complete	Indicates the completion of the called party number
Transit network selection	Identifies a transit network (an IXC in the United States)
Endpoint reference	Identifies endpoints in a point-to-multipoint connection
Endpoint state	Indicates state of each endpoint (add party initiated, received, active, etc.)
Restart indicator	Identifies which virtual channels are to be restated

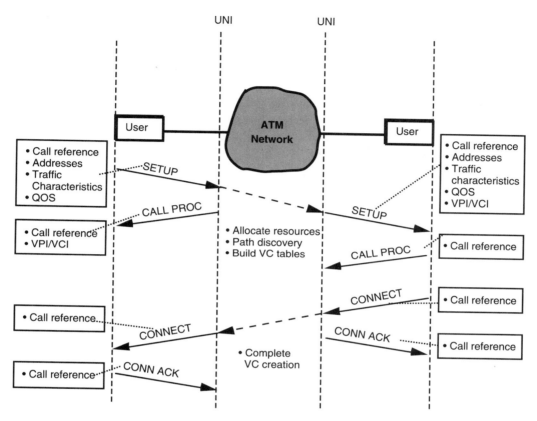

Figure 7–3   Connection setup.

user. This message contains several information elements (fields) to: (a) identify the message, (b) specify various AAL parameters, (c) identify the calling and called party addresses, (d) establish requirements for QOS, (e) select the transit network (if needed), and (f) specify a number of other requirements.

Upon receiving the SETUP message, the network returns a CALL PROCEEDING message to the initiating user, forwards the SETUP message to the called user, and waits for the called user to return a CALL PROCEEDING message. The CALL PROCEEDING message is used to indicate that the call has been initiated and no more call establishment information is needed, nor will any be accepted.

The called user, if it accepts a call, will then send to the network a CONNECT message. This CONNECT message will then be forwarded to the calling user. The CONNECT message contains parameters that deal with some of the same parameters in the SETUP message such as call reference and message type, as well as the accepted AAL parameters and several other identifiers that are created as a result of the information elements in the original SETUP message.

Upon receiving the CONNECT messages, the calling user and the network return the CONNECT ACKNOWLEDGE to their respective parties.

Either user can initiate a disconnect operation (see Figure 7–4). To do so requires the user to send the RELEASE message to the network. This message clears the end-to-end connection between the two users and the network. This message only contains the basic information to identify the message across the network. Other parameters are not included because they are not needed to clear the state tables for the connection.

The receiving network and receiving user are required to transmit the RELEASE COMPLETE message as a result of receiving the RELEASE message.

The Q.2931 Timers

The vast majority of networks that provide connections on demand use timers at both the user and network nodes to define reasonable wait periods for completion of certain actions (such as completion of a setup,

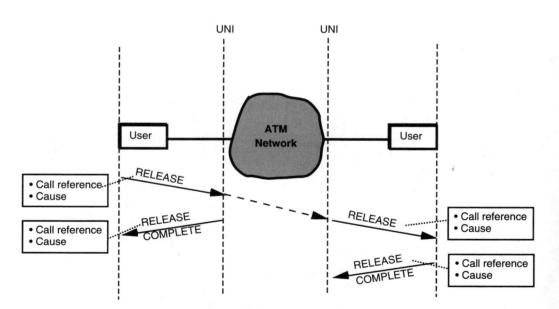

Figure 7–4   Connection release.

completion of a restart, etc.). The ATM UNI signaling interface provides ten timers at the network side and ten timers at the user side (see Table 7–3).

Each connection is controlled by states. For example, a user enters into a "call present" state when a call establishment request has been received but the user has not yet responded to the request. Various states can be entered and exited as a call is processed, some of which are governed by timers. In the event an action does not take place before a designated timer expires, various remedial actions are dictated, such as issuing retries or moving to other states.

Table 7–3 Timers

Timer Network Side	Number User Side	Cause for Start	Normal Stop
T301		Not supported in this Implementation Agreement	
T303	T303	SETUP sent	CONNECT, CALL PROCEEDING, or RELEASE COMPLETE received
T308	T308	RELEASE sent	RELEASE COMPLETE or RELEASE received
T309	T309	SAAL disconnection	SAAL reconnected
T310	T310	CALL PROCEEDING received	CONNECT or RELEASE received
	T313	CONNECT sent	CONNECT ACKNOW-LEDGE received
T316	T316	RESTART sent	RESTART ACKNOW-LEDGE received
T317	T317	RESTART received	Internal clearing of call references
T322	T322	STATUS ENQUIRY sent	STATUS, RELEASE, or RELEASE COMPLETE received
T398	T398	DROP PARTY sent	DROP PARTY ACKNOWLEDGE or RELEASE received
T399	T399	ADD PARTY sent	ADD PARTY ACKNOWLEDGE, ADD PARTY REJECT or RELEASE received

THE UNI OPERATIONS IN MORE DETAIL

We continue our analysis of the Q.2931 UNI with a more detailed examination of the operations. In this section, I show how the Q.2931 timers and the parameters in the messages are used. I will focus on all the mandatory parameters and several optional parameters that warrant our interest.

The Connection Establishment Operation

Figure 7–5 shows the timers invoked for the establishment of a connection. Three timers are involved in the process and perform the following functions.

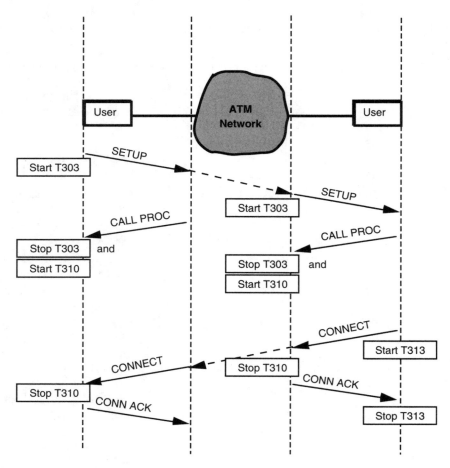

Figure 7–5   The connection setup procedure.

Timer T303 is invoked when ATM issues a SETUP message to the network on the local side of the network and is invoked by network node at the remote side when it passes the SETUP message to the user. The timer is stopped when the remote end user returns a CALL PROCEEDING message. This message is relayed to the local network side, which also sends it to the originating user. Although not illustrated in this figure, timer T303 can also be stopped if either a CONNECT message or a RELEASE COMPLETE message is received. If the timer expires before the reception of a CALL PROCEEDING message, a SETUP message may be retransmitted or, if the network does not support SETUP retransmissions, the potential connection is cleared and a null state is entered. The ATM specifications require that only one retry may be attempted after which a null state must be entered.

Upon receiving the CALL PROCEEDING message, the local user and remote network node turn off their T303 timers and turn on their T310 timers. This timer waits for the CONNECT message to be sent to either party. Upon successful reception of the CONNECT message, timer T310 is turned off and the recipients of this message respond with a CONNECTION ACKNOWLEDGMENT of this message. If the CONNECTION ACKNOWLEDGMENT message is not received before timer T310 expires, the connection must be cleared.

The remote user also invokes timer T313 when it sends the CONNECT message to the network. This timer is turned off upon receiving the CONNECT ACKNOWLEDGMENT message.

The SETUP message must contain all the information required for the network and the called party to process the call. This information must include the QOS parameters, the cell rate parameters, and any bearer capabilities that the network may need at either side. The user is not allowed to fill in the connection identifier information element in the SETUP message. If it is included, the network ignores it. This means that the network selects the VPI/VCI for the connection. This information is returned to the user in the CALL PROCEEDING message.

A similar procedure is performed on the remote side of the network in that the network node is responsible for allocating the VPI/VCI value and placing this value in the SETUP message before it sends this message to the called user.

The Connection Release Operation

The connection release operation entails only timer T308 (see Figure 7–6). Either the network or the user can invoke the connection release by sending the RELEASE message to the respective party. This op-

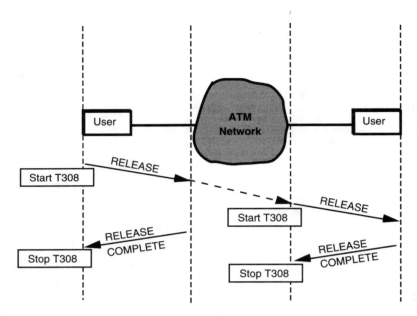

Figure 7–6   The release procedure.

eration turns on timer T308 which remains on until the RELEASE message is received. If T308 expires for the first time, the RELEASE message is retransmitted. If a response is not returned on this second try, the user must release the call reference and return to the null state (no connection exists). The manner in which this operation is then handled is not defined in the standard but is network or user specific.

In the event that a RELEASE message is received by the network or the user at the same time that the respective node sends a RELEASE (this procedure is called a clear-clear collision), the affected party stops timer T308 and releases the call reference as well as the virtual channel and enters into the null state.

The Restart Operation

The network or user can initiate restart operations for any number of reasons (see Figure 7–7). Failure of any component can result in the restart procedure being invoked, and information elements in the header cite the reason for the restart. The initiation of the restart invokes timer T316 by the originator sending the RESTART message to the recipient. In turn, the recipient starts timer T317 upon receiving the RESTART message. After processing the RESTART message and taking any neces-

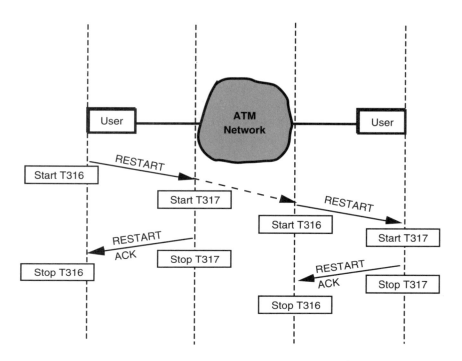

Figure 7–7   The restart operation.

sary actions, the recipient issues a RESTART acknowledge and stops
T317. A RESTART acknowledge is sent to the originator, which then
stops T316. The field in the RESTART message labeled restart indicator
determines if an indicated virtual channel is to be restarted or all channels controlled by this layer 3 entity are to be restarted.

The Status Inquiry Operation

The status inquiry procedure depicted in Figure 7–8 is invoked by
either the network or the user to determine the state of a connection,
such as the call state, the type of connection being supported, the end
state of a point-to-multipoint connection, and so on. As indicated in this
figure, timer T322 controls this procedure. Either party may invoke the
STATUS INQUIRY message by turning T322 on. Upon receipt of the
STATUS or STATUS COMPLETE message, this timer is turned off.

The Add Party Operation

Because of the importance and wide use of telephone conference calls,
multicasting data traffic, and video conferencing operations, the ATM de-

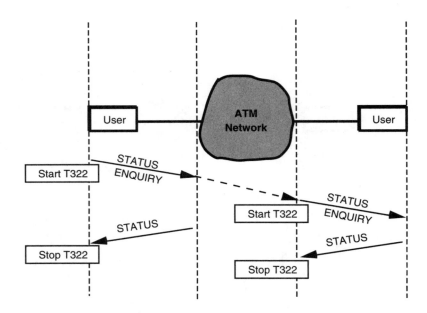

Figure 7–8   The status enquiry operation.

signers developed procedures to support these types of applications. It is anticipated that most initial implementations will be data only.

This capability is implemented through the add-party procedure as shown in Figure 7–9. This illustration shows the addition of only one party, but multiple parties may be connected with this operation. The originating site issues an ADD PARTY message across the UNI to the network. The network forwards this message to the destination in which the destination network node issues a SETUP across the UNI to the destination user. The SETUP message is used if procedures must begin from scratch. That is to say, this UNI is currently not participating in the call. Not shown in this figure is the possibility of issuing the ADD PARTY message across the remote UNI for situations where a call is already in place and another calling party needs to be added.

The operation is controlled with timer T399 at the sending site. This timer is turned off upon receiving a CONNECTION ACKNOWLEDG-MENT, an ADD PARTY, ADD PARTY ACK, REJECT, or a RELEASE. In this example, the remote side uses the initial setup operation, dis-cussed earlier. The point-to-multipoint operation is also controlled by party-states. These states may exist on the network side or the user side of the interface. They are summarized as follows:

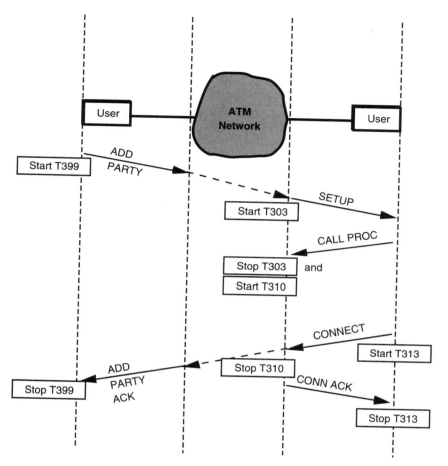

Figure 7–9   The add party procedure.

- *Null:* A party does not exist; therefore an endpoint reference value has not been allocated.
- *Add party initiated:* An ADD PARTY message or a SETUP message has been sent to the other side of the interface for this party.
- *Add party received:* An ADD PARTY message or a setup message has been received by the other side of the interface for this party.
- *Drop party initiated:* A DROP PARTY message has been sent for this party.
- *Drop party received:* A DROP PARTY message has been received for this party.
- *Active:* On the user side of the UNI, an active state is when the

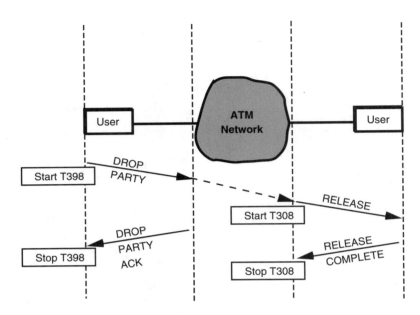

Figure 7–10   The drop party procedure.

user has received an CONNECT ACKNOWLEDGE, ADD PARTY ACKNOWLEDGE, or a CONNECT. On the network side, an active state is entered when it has sent a CONNECT, CONNECT ACKNOWLEDGE, or an ADD PARTY ACKNOWLEDGE, or when the network has received an ADD PARTY ACKNOWLEDGE from the user side.

The Drop Party Operation

As the reader might expect, the drop party operations provide the opposite function of the add party procedure discussed in the previous section (see Figure 7–10). With this operation, one party or multiple parties can be dropped from the connection. The activity is controlled by the T398 and T308 timers. In this example, the RELEASE and RELEASE COMPLETE messages are used at the remote side. Under certain conditions the drop party is also activated at the remote side.

THE Q.931 MESSAGE INFORMATION ELEMENTS IN MORE DETAIL

This section explains the Q.2931 information elements that are mandatory and those that are optional but are needed to support several important operations. The structure of the elements is illustrated in several figures, but I have not described all the coding rules and bit-structure of the information elements. This practice is in keeping with the overall theme of the book, and the reader should study *ATM Forum User-Network Interface Specification* (V.4.0) and ITU-T Q.2931 if more detal is needed.

AAL Information Element

Figure 7–11 illustrates the first 6 octets of the AAL information element. These octets are used for all AAL types. Octet 1 is coded as 01011000 to identify the information element. Octet 2 is preset or not significant. Octet 5 is coded to indicate the AAL type information that follows in octets 6 through n:

00000001   AAL type 1
00000011   AAL type 3/4
00000101   AAL type 5
00010000   User-defined AAL

AAL Type 1.   Figure 7–12 shows the information elements for octet groups 6–12 for AAL type 1. The subtype identifier indicates:

00000000   Null/empty
00000001   Voice-band 64 kbit/s

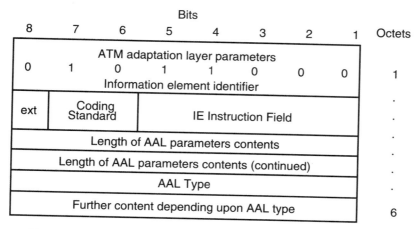

Figure 7–11   AAL information element for all AAL types.

Bits

8	7	6	5	4	3	2	1	Octets

									6
Subtype identifer								
Subtype								
CBR Rate Identifier								
CBR Rate								
Multiplier Identifier								
Multiplier (Note 1)								
Multiplier (continued)								
Source Clock Frequency Recovery Method Identifier								
Source Clock Frequency Recovery Method								
Error Correction Method Identifier								
Error Correction Method								
Structured Data Transfer Blocksize Identifier								
Structured Data Transfer Blocksize								
Partially Filled Cells Identifier								
Partially Filled Cells Method								n

These octets are only present if CBR rate indicates "n x 64 kbit/s".

Figure 7–12   Information elements for an AAL Type 1 connection.

00000010   Circuit emulation (synchronous)
00000011   Circuit emulation (asynchronous)
00000100   High-quality audio
00000101   Video

The CBR rate requests a bit rate for the session. It is coded as follows:

00000001   64 kbit/s
00000100   1544 kbit/s (DS1)
00000101   6312 kbit/s (DS2)

00000110	32064 kbit/s
00000111	44736 kbit/s (DS3)
00001000	97728 kbit/s
00010000	2048 kbit/s (E1)
00010001	8448 kbit/s (E2)
00010010	34368 kbit/s (E3)
00010011	139264 kbit/s (E4)
01000000	$n \times 64$ kbit/s

The multiplier parameter is used to define a $n \times 64$ kbit/s, with n ranging from 2 to $2^{16} - 1$. The clock recovery type parameter indicates the kind of clocking operation to be employed to recover and decode the signal (timestamp, etc.). The error correction parameter identifies the type of error correction method employed to detect errors at the terminating endpoint (none, FEC, etc.). The structured data transfer identifies that this connection will or will not use structured data transfer. The partially filled cells parameter states how many of the 47 octets in the cell are in use.

AAL Type 3/4.   Figure 7–13 shows the parameters for AAL types 3/4 and 5 The functions represented in these fields were explained previously. Briefly, then, the service specific CS (SSCS) and the common part of CS (CPCS) parameters indicate (1) the maximum CPCS-SDU sizes (forward and backward), with values ranging from 1 to 65,535 ($2^{16} - 1$); (2) the ranges for the message identification field (1 to 1023); (3) a message or streaming mode; and (4) SSCS type (such assured operations, a frame relay SSCS, etc.).

Broadband Low Layer Informaton Element

Figure 7–14 shows the parameters of the broadband low layer information element. The mode field defines if extended (0–127) or normal sequencing (0–7) is to be employed at layer 2 (if sequencing is employed). The Q.933 field is used, based on implementation-specific rules. The window size field (k) can range from 1–127.

The next parameters define if user-specified layer 2 and layer 3 protocols are employed. The mode field defines if extended (0–127) or normal sequencing (0–7) is to be employed at layer 3 (if sequencing is employed). The default packet size field is used to define the default size of the X.25 packet (if X.25 is invoked). The packet window size is also employed for X.25 for a range of 1–127.

AAL Type 3/4

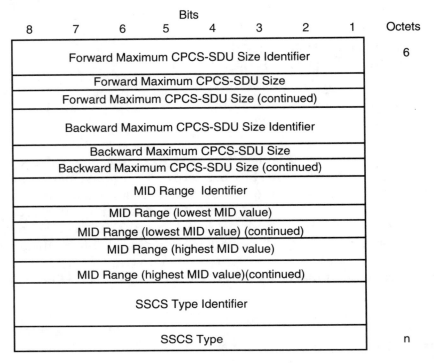

AAL Type 5

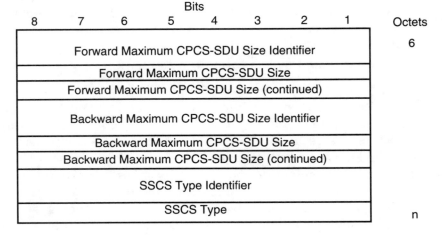

Figure 7–13   Parameters for AAL Types 3/4 and 5.

Bits

8	7	6	5	4	3	2	1	Octets
Broadband low layer information								1
ext	Coding Standard		IE Instruction Field					.
Length of B-LLI contents								.
Length of B-LLI contents (continued)								.
ext	Layer 1 id		User information layer 1 protocol					.
ext	Layer 2 id		User information layer 2 protocol					.
ext	Mode		Spare			Q.933 use		.
ext	Window size (k)							.
ext	User specified layer 2 protocol information							.
ext	Layer 3 id		User information layer 3 protocol					.
ext	Mode		Spare					.
ext	Spare			Default Packet Size				.
ext	Packet window size							.
ext	User specified layer 3 protocol information							.
ext	ISO/IEC TR 9577 Initial Protocol Identifier (IPI)							.
ext	IPI		Spare					.
ext	SNAP ID		Spare					.
OUI Octet 1								.
OUI Octet 2								.
OUI Octet 3								.
PID Octet 1								.
PID Octet 2								n

Figure 7–14   The broadband low layer information element.

The remainder of the octets in this information element can be used to identify Subnetwork Access Protocol (SNAP) information. If so indicated by octets 7a, a 24-bit organization unique ID (OUI) and a 16-bit protocol ID (PID) are contained in the last octets of the information element. The OUI and PID are values that are registered under ISO, the IEEE, and the Internet.

ATM FORUM UNI VERSION 4.0 VARIATIONS

The ITU-T specifications do not allow a leaf to joint an ADD PARTY Connection without the intervention of the root. The ATM Forum UNI establishes procedures for the leaf to initiate an ADD PARTY request, which is handled by the network. The root is not involved in this operation. This operation is called the leaf initiated join capability (LIJ).

UNI 4.0 also provides for an ATM group address, which is a collection of ATM end systems. The idea of the group address is to identify related end stations that provide well known services (for example, ATM LAN emulation services).

Group addressing also allows an ATM end system to define a membership scope during the address registration procedure, which is used to determine the range of routing. For example, a limited scope can restrict routing to a single Ethernet network (including bridges and repeaters).[1]

In conjunction with group addressing, version 4.0 defines the Anycast operation. This procedure allows a single ATM end system to request a point-to-point connection to a single ATM end system that is part of an ATM group.

SUMMARY

Broadband signaling at the UNI establishes call and connection control operations and defines how connections are set up on demand between users and the ATM network. The Q.2931 connection control protocol, based on the ISDN Q.931, is used for these operations.

Q.2931 utilizes the OSI address syntax and supports point-to-point, point-to-multipoint, and multipoint-to-multipoint connections.

---

[1]As explained later in this book the most limited scope would correlate to the bottom level of the PNNI routing heirarchy.

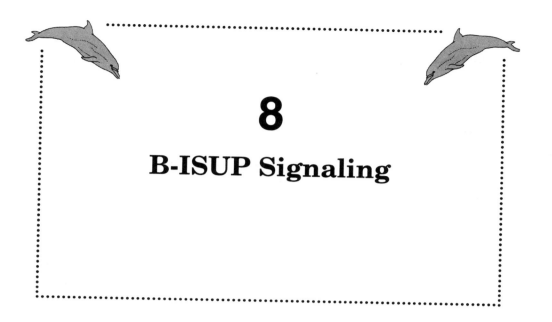

8

B-ISUP Signaling

INTRODUCTION

This chapter examines the Broadband ISDN user part (B-ISUP), one of the key applications used in a broadband signaling network. The relationships of B-ISUP, ISUP, and SS7 are explained, as well as how they interwork with each other. The B-ISUP entities (sublayers) are examined as well, and due to the close relationships of these B-ISUP entities, it will be necessary to examine the primitives that are exchanged between them.

The ANSI T1.648 and ITU-T Q.2764 and Q.2763 standards are examined in this chapter. They are quite similar to each other and I will point out their major differences during this analysis.

A few more comments before we proceed. The UNI and NNI message parameters are closely associated with each other. Therefore, I have included this information as Appendix 8A and will not repeat the descriptions of the parameters that are the same, but will refer you to Chapter 7. Finally, the interfaces and primitives between the B-ISUP entities are quite varied and complex and might be of interest only to the reader who is a programmer. I describe the major aspects of these operations in one section of this chapter and provide more details in Appendix 8B.

PURPOSE OF B-ISUP

The principal function of B-ISUP is to provide the signaling functions necessary to set up, manage, and terminate a virtual circuit in the broadband network. It provides functions to support both basic bearer and supplementary services and is based on ISUP. In addition, ANSI B-ISUP is based on (with some minor exceptions) the same procedures as the ITU-T specifications that are published in ITU-T Recommendations Q.276, Q.2764 and Q.2730.

As its name implies, B-ISUP is related to ISUP, and draws most of its features from its narrowband counterpart. The B-ISUP developers took this approach because ISUP has proven to be an effective signaling protocol, and many designers and programmers have used it. It makes little sense to start from scratch when existing technology can be modified to accomplish the job.

Like ISUP, B-ISUP is designed to transfer control information between elements in a telecommunications network. The principal elements are switches, but B-ISUP can operate between other signaling points as well, such as operations centers and switches and their associated databases. The control information is used to establish and terminate virtual circuits and to manage the bandwidth of the virtual circuits.

WHAT B-ISUP DOES NOT DO

While B-ISUP is the mechanism for transferring signaling information between network nodes, it does *not* become involved in the following operations:

- Bandwidth capacity analysis (at the network nodes)
- Path discovery through the network (and through the network nodes)
- Setting up the routing and mapping tables (cross-connect tables) for the virtual circuits
- Ongoing operations, administration, and maintenance (OAM) of the existing virtual circuits

The first two operations are not defined in any of the broadband signaling standards and are left to the network operator and switch supplier to implement. The Internet RFC 1695 provides a model for building cross-connect tables, and separate standards deal with OAM (these two subjects are discussed in Volume I of this series). We will spend a few moments here on the subjects of bandwidth analysis and path discovery.

Bandwidth Analysis and Path Discovery

In order for a broadband network to support the rapid setup of a connection, it must have a means to know quite quickly which network nodes can or cannot support the connection. The best approach to set up connections in a timely manner is for the nodes to perform ongoing bandwidth analysis and path discovery with each other. The nodes send messages to each other about their spare capacity and capability to support connections. The messages may be exchanged on a periodic basis or when a node experiences an unusual condition, such as reaching a threshold in its utilization.

It is also possible for bandwidth determination to be made upon receiving a call request from a user, with each successive node requesting bandwidth from its downstream neighbor until a complete path has been set up between the calling and called parties. This approach entails more delay in setting up the connection but cuts down on the number of messages that must be exchanged in comparison to an ongoing analysis.

Assuming path discovery has been an ongoing process, when the originating node (originating exchange) receives a Q.2931 SETUP message from a user, it is aware of the ability (or inability) of the other network nodes to support the connection. When this exchange sends a B-ISUP "setup" message to a neighboring node, it knows that its neighbor exchange can support the connection, since these nodes have been keeping each other informed about their ongoing operations.

These types of operations are often called route advertisements, or route discovery, and are a common aspect of most advanced networks. Some networks have moved to the use of a link state protocol, known generally as a shortest path first (SPF). The term is inaccurate; a better term is optimum path, but the former term is now accepted. These protocols are based on well-tested techniques that have been used in the industry for a number of years.

Ideally, communications networks are designed to route user traffic based on a variety of criteria, generally referred to as a least-cost routing. The name does not mean that routing is based solely on obtaining the least-cost route in the literal sense. Other factors are often part of a network routing algorithm, and for broadband networks, advertising bandwidth availability and delay are key parts of the advertisement.

Even though networks vary in least-cost criteria, three constraints must be considered: (1) delay, (2) throughput, and (3) connectivity. If delay is excessive or if throughput is too little, the network does not meet the needs of the user community. The third constraint is quite obvious; the exchanges must be able to reach each other; otherwise, all other least-cost criteria are irrelevant.

POSITION OF B-ISUP IN THE BROADBAND SIGNALING LAYERS

Previously, we examined the overall architecture of broadband signaling networks, which included a description of where B-ISUP fits into this architecture. The reader may wish to review Figures 6–1, 6–2, and 6–3.

THE SS7 MTP SUPPORT TO B-ISUP

B-ISDN is a fundamental part of SS7 architecture and relies on MTP 3 for support services. B-ISUP and MTP 3 interact through conventional OSI primitives. The information transferred between these protocols is summarized in Figure 8–1 and Table 8–1. Only request and indication primitives are invoked and only four primitives are needed for

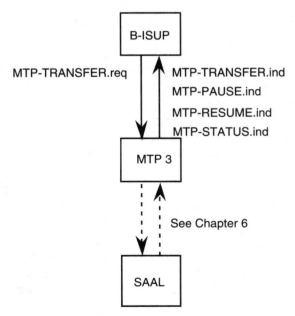

Figure 8–1   MTP 3 and B-ISUP interface.

Table 8-1 MTP 3 and B-ISUP Primitives

Primitive	Req	Ind	Res	Con	Parameters
MTP-TRANSFER	x	x			OPC, DPC, SLS, SIO, signaling information
MTP-PAUSE		x			Affected DPC
MTP-RESUME		x			Affected DPC
MTP-STATUS		x			Affected DPC, cause

B-ISUP to obtain the services of MTP 3. A brief description of the primitives follows.

The MTP_TRANSFER primitive is used by B-ISUP (request) to obtain the message handling functions of MTP 3 and by MTP 3 (indication) to deliver signaling information to B-ISUP. Both primitives contain the originating point code (OPC), destination point code (DPC), signaling link selection code (SLS), service information octet (SIO), and signaling information, which is discussed later in this chapter.

The MTP-PAUSE is sent only as an indication primitive by MTP 3 to inform B-ISUP that MTP 3 is not able to transfer messages to the specified DPC.

The MTP_RESUME is also sent only as an indication primitive by MTP 3 to inform B-ISUP that MTP 3 has resumed its ability to transfer messages to the specified DPC.

As shown in Table 8-1, the MTP_PAUSE and MTP_RESUME primitives contain only one parameter, the affected DPC.

The MTP_STATUS primitive is sent by MTP 3 as an indication primitive to B-ISUP to specify that a signaling route is congested or the destination B-ISUP is not available. The primitive contains the affected DPC and cause parameter that identifies: (1) the signaling network is congested, (2) the User Part is unavailable because a remote user is unequipped, (3) the user is inaccessible, or (4) the User Part is unavailable for unknown reasons.

OVERVIEW OF THE B-ISUP OPERATIONS

Q.2931 and B-ISUP are separate protocols, and they perform different operations in the signaling network architecture. But they are "partners" in that Q.2931 assumes B-ISUP will set up the virtual connections within a network, and B-ISUP assumes Q.2931 will set up the virtual

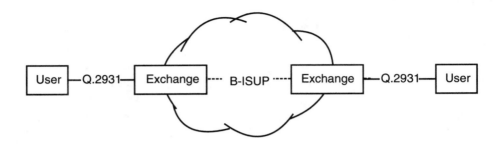

Figure 8–2   Relationship of Q.2931 and B-ISUP.

connections at the network boundaries (outside the network). As depicted in Figure 8–2, Q.2931 is viewed as a user-network interface (UNI) operating between the user device and the network node, and B-ISUP is viewed as part of the network-node interface (NNI) operating between the nodes within the network.

Trunk Groups and VPCIs

The "trunk group" is a key concept in narrowband signaling. It consists of one or more trunks that connect two switches. In ATM broadband signaling, a virtual path connection (VPC) is analogous to a narrowband trunk group. The VPC is assigned a specified amount of bandwidth, which may be an entire link (say, an OC-3) or a subset of it (part of an OC-3).

To allocate and identify bandwidth for SVCs, the concept of a virtual path connection identifier (VPCI) is used. The VPCI identifies the specific VPC that is used for a connection—it must be unique over a particular destination point code (DPC) and originating point code (OPC) combination within the broadband signaling system. There must be a unique VPCI and VPI at a physical interface.

Therefore, a VPCI/DPC/OPC is defined as the broadband equivalent of a narrowband trunk group, and the broadband equivalent of a narrowband channel is the virtual channel, which is identified by the VCI. The VCI needs to be unique only within a VPCI.

In a narrowband system, an idle trunk must be available within a trunk group before a connection is granted and, once granted, the bandwidth is fixed. In the broadband system, there is no fixed bandwidth for a VCI, although the total number of VCIs associated with each VPCI cannot exceed the allocated bandwidth for that VPCI.

Setting up the Virtual Circuits

B-ISUP is responsible for assigning bandwidth to connections in the network, putting routes into service, and managing the VPCI/VCI values for these connections. These procedures include the following activities.

Before a route is put into service between two exchanges, the VPCIs to be used are assigned unambiguously and identically at both ends of each VPC. For every VPCI, B-ISUP defines which exchange controls this VPCI. This exchange is responsible for assigning bandwidth and the VPCI/VCI for this VPCI.

B-ISUP uses a default mechanism that is defined for determining this designation. Each exchange will be the assigning exchange for one-half of the VPCI values. The exchange with the higher signaling point code will be the assigning exchange for all even numbered VPCI values, and the other exchange will be the assigning exchange for all odd numbered VPCI values.

The assigning exchange must perform the following actions:

- From several available VPCs, it must select one VPC that is able to provide the requested bandwidth according to the requested ATM cell rate.
- It must assign bandwidth and a VCI value to the call/connection, and it must update the bandwidth and VCI value of the selected VPCI.

The *assigning* exchange assigns both VPCI/VCI and bandwidth (according to its connection admission control (CAC) procedures for outgoing and incoming calls. The non-assigning exchange does not assign but requests the assigning exchange to assign both VPCI/VCI and bandwidth.

The virtual circuits must undergo a VPCI/VCI consistency check in order to verify the correct allocation of a VPCI to an interface in both of the connected exchanges. This check uses the loopback F4 flow described in Volume I of this series (and specified in ITU-T I.610).

B-ISUP NNI MESSAGES AND PARAMETERS

This section provides an overview of B-ISUP and the parameters in these messages. After they are described, we will provide several examples of how B-ISUP uses these messages to support users' connections in the broadband network.

The Messages

This section provides an summary description of the B-ISUP messages, which are listed in Table 8–2. For ease of reference, they are listed in alphabetical order.

Address Complete Message (ACM).   This message is sent in the backward direction to indicate that all addressing information has been

Table 8–2   B-ISUP Messages

Address complete (ACM)

Answer (ANM)

Blocking (BLO)

Blocking acknowledgment (BLA)

Call progress (CPG)

Confusion (CFN)

Consistency check end (CCE)

Consistency check request acknowledgment (CCEA)

Consistency check request (CSR)

Exit (EXM) (2)

Forward transfer (FOT)

IAM acknowledgment (IAA)

IAM reject (IAR)

Initial address (IAM)

Network resource management (NRM) (1)

Release (REL)

Release complete (RLC)

Reset (RSM)

Reset acknowledgment (RAM)

Resume (RES)

Segmentation (SGM)

Subsequent address (SAM) (1)

Suspend (SUS)

Unblocking (UBL)

Unblocking acknowledgment (UBA)

User part available (UPA)

User part test (UPT)

User-to-user information (USR) (1)

(1) Defined in the ITU-T Q.2763; not in the ANSI T1.648
(2) Defined in the ANSI T1.648, not in the ITU-T Q.2763

received to complete the call to the called party. It also conveys that the call is being processed.

Answer Message (ANM).   This message is sent in the backward direction to indicate that the called party has answered the call.

Blocking Message (BLO). This message is typically used for maintenance purposes and is sent to the exchange at the other end of the virtual circuit to block outgoing calls at that remote end. The affected exchange should still be able to receive incoming calls on the affected resource.

Blocking Acknowledgment Message (BLA). This message acknowledges the BLO and signals that the resource has been blocked.

Call Progress Message (CPG).   This message indicates that an event has occurred in the processing of a call. It can be sent in the forward or backward direction and usually indicates that the call is being processed without problems.

Confusion Message (CFN). This message is a catch-all (which most software-based systems have) that is sent by an exchange in response to receiving a message that it does not understand (either the message, the fields in the message, or both).

Consistency Check Request End Message (CCE).   This message terminates the consistency check operation and the ATM cell monitoring operations.

Consistency Check Acknowledgment Message (CCEA). This message is sent in response to the consistency check request message.

Consistency Check Request Message (CSR). This message requests that the other end of the virtual connection verify the correct VPCI for a VP. The message requires that receiving exchange activate an ATM cell monitoring operation.

Exit Message (EXM).   This message is sent by an outgoing gateway exchange in the backward direction to signal that call setup has occurred successfully to the adjacent network. The message is exchanged only within a network.

Forward Transfer Message (FOT). This message in sent in the forward direction on semi-automatic calls when the assistance of an operator is needed. The operator may be recalled when the call is completed.

IAM Acknowledgment Message (IAA). This message is sent in response to an initial address message to indicate that resources are available, the IAM has been accepted, and that the requested bandwidth (on this incoming leg, for both directions) is available.

IAM Reject Message (IAR). This message is sent in response to an initial address message to indicate that the call is refused due to the unavailability of resources.

Initial Address Message (IAM). This message is the first message sent to begin the call connection process. It initiates the seizure of the outgoing virtual circuit.

Network Resource Management Message (NRM). This message is used to convey echo control information.

Release Message (REL). This message is sent (in either direction) to begin the release of the circuit, and to free the resources that had been reserved for the connection.

Release Complete Message (RLC). This message acknowledges the REL message. It indicates that the virtual circuit has been released.

Reset Message (RSM). If an exchange loses its knowledge about the state of a connection (register problem, memory loss, signaling identifier, whatever), it sends this message to the far-end exchange (in either direction).

Reset Acknowledgment Message (RAM). This message acknowledges the RSM.

Resume Message (RES). This message is sent in the backward direction and is used to indicate that a calling or called party has been reconnected after having been suspended.

Segmentation Message (SGM). In the event a message must be divided into smaller parts, this message indicates that it is part of the original oversize message.

Subsequent Address Message (SAM). This message is used if a subsequent number is to be passed to a node.

Suspend Message (SUS). This message indicates that the calling or called party has been temporarily suspended.

Unblocking Message (UBL). This message unblocks the resource that was blocked by the blocking message (BLO).

Unblocking Acknowledgment Message (UBA). This message acknowledges the UBL and indicates that the resource is unblocked.

User Part Available Message (UPA). This message acknowledges the user part test message (UPT).

User Part Test Message (UPT). B-ISUP can test entities to determine if a particular user part is available. This message is sent to an exchange to make this test.

User-to-User Information Message (USR). This message is used to pass information between the users, but not to any network node.

Parameters in the Messages

One could ask why yet another protocol has been defined for signaling when the conventional ISUP for the narrowband NNI is already written and in operation. Indeed, some people (developers of products that use these protocols) have complained that ISUP could have been modified to handle any special signaling needs for a broadband network. That is exactly what happened with ISUP; it was modified and named B-ISUP to distinguish it from the narrowband ISUP counterpart.

We shall see that B-ISUP is needed because it carries parameters that do not pertain to a conventional circuit-based network, on which ISUP operates. Likewise, ISUP carries parameters that are not pertinent to a virtual circuit-based network. Appendix 8A (at the end of this chapter) provides a summary of the parameters that are carried in the B-ISUP messages. Some of them are mapped transparently from Q.2931 to B-ISUP at the ingress node to the network and back to Q.2931 at the egress node. These parameters are described in Chapter 7. The next section shows a example of B-ISUP operations and will explain how some of the more widely used parameters are employed.

EXAMPLES OF B-ISUP OPERATIONS

Figure 8–3 shows the flow of messages that occur in a typical call setup between two exchanges. Several to many parameters can be coded into these messages. I describe those that are of the most importance for the call and, as just mentioned, Appendix 8A explains each parameter. Table 8–3 lists

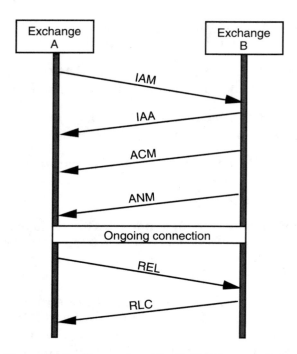

Figure 8–3   Examples of a B-ISUP operation.

and describes the timers used in B-ISUP operations, and several will be explained in this section. The "Timer Expires" column lists the actions that occur when the timer is not turned off by receipt of the expected message.

The operations begin when exchange A issues an initial address message (IAM). During this procedure, exchange A assigns an origination signaling id (OSID) for this side of the connection and turns on timer T40b.

Also during this operation, the virtual circuit is set up along an appropriate route. The decisions on how a route is selected is not defined by B-ISUP, but is left to the discretion of the B-ISUP implementor. However the route is chosen, its selection must depend on the parameters furnished to it by the user. These parameters are the called party number, broadband bearer capability, ATM cell rate, and—if the maximum end-to-end transit delay parameter is used—the propagation delay counter must also be considered. Other parameters can be placed in this message and/or sent unaltered to the end destination. These include: AAL parameters, broadband bearer capability (as we just learned, also used for route selection), broadband low layer information, broadband high layer information, narrowband high layer compatibility, narrowband low layer compatibility, OAM traffic descriptor, and progress indicator.

Table 8–3   The B-ISUP Timers

Name (Symbol)	Timer Started	Timer Stopped	Timer Expires
Await Release Complete (T1b)	When Release message is sent	Receipt of Release Complete Message	Release resources, alert maintenance and send Reset message
User Part Availability (T4b)	At receipt of MTP-STATUS primitive coded with cause "remote user unavailable"	Receipt of User Part Available message	Send User Part Test message and start T4b
Await Network Resume (T6b)	When controlling network receives Suspend message	At the receipt of Resume or Release message	Initiate release procedure
Await Address Complete (T7b)	When the latest address message is sent	At the receipt of Address complete, Answer messages	Release all equipment and connection and send Release message
Await answer (T9b)	Exchange receives Address Complete message	At the receipt of Answer message	Release connection and send Release message
Await Blocking Acknowledge (T12b)	When Blocking message is sent	At receipt of Blocking Acknowledgment	Alert Maintenance system
Await Unblocking Acknowledge (T14b)	When Unblocking message is sent	At receipt of Unblocking Acknowledgment	Alert Maintenance system
Await Reset Acknowledge (T16b)	When Reset message is sent	At receipt of Reset Acknowledgment message	Resend Reset message
Repeat Reset (T17b)	When Reset Acknowledgment is not received within timer "Await Reset Acknowledgment"		Resend Reset message, alert maintenance
Segmentation (T34b)	When indication of a segmented message is received	At receipt of a segmentation message	Proceed with call
Await Network Resume-International (T38b)	When the incoming international exchange sends to the preceding exchange a Suspend (network) message	At Receipt of Resume (network) message or Release message	Send Release message

(continued)

Table 8–3   Continued

Name (Symbol)	Timer Started	Timer Stopped	Timer Expires
Await IAM Acknowledge (T40b)	When Initial Address Message is sent	At receipt of IAM Acknowledgment or IAM Reject	Release resources, alert maintenance system, send Reset message
Await Consistency Check Request Acknowledgment (T41b)	When Consistency Check Request message is sent	At receipt of Consistency Check Request Acknowledgment	Alert Maintenance system
Await Consistency Check end Acknowledgment (T42b)	When Consistency Check End message is sent	At receipt of Consistency Check End Acknowledgment	Alert Maintenance system

The calling party number may be included depending on the implementation and is subject to bilateral agreements among networks. If present, it may be used for address screening.

When the IAM arrives at exchange B, this exchange must perform the VPCI/VCI assignments and allocate bandwidth. Of course, these operations assume the called party number is valid and the called party can be connected. If the connection is allowed, exchange B will offer the call to the called party.

In addition, upon successful receipt of the IAM at exchange B, this exchange assigns an origination signaling id (OSID). Therefore, exchange A and exchange B each have assigned an OSID to this connection. These values will be used hereafter to keep track of this specific connection.

Upon successful assignment procedures and other processing at exchange B, this exchange returns an IAM acknowledge message (IAA) to exchange A. The IAA message contains: (1) a connection element id, (2) the destination signaling id (which is the OSID assigned by exchange A), and (3) the origination signaling id (which is the OSID assigned by B). The connection element id contains the VPCI and the VCI. Also, the receipt of IAA results in turning off timer T40b.

At exchange B, the address complete message (ACM) is issued to exchange A to indicate that the IAM is complete and sufficient to process the call. Several parameters are coded in the ACM; some of the more significant ones are the backward narrowband interworking indicators, the called party's indicators, the charge indicator, and the destination signaling indicator. At exchange A, the receipt of the ACM turns on timer T9b.

When the called party answers, exchange B removes ringing tone from the line (if applicable) and sends the answer message (ANM) to the originating exchange. As this message transits from exchange B to exchange A, any resources at intermediate exchanges that were in a "wait state" must be activated. For example, cross-connect tables containing entries about the virtual connection must have these entries set to "active." As a general statement, the ANM operation results in resources in the network being reserved for the virtual connection, but they may not be activated until the ANM is received from the terminating exchange. After the ANM is received at exchange A, the bidirectional virtual circuit is open to both the called and calling parties, and the exchange of information can begin. The receipt of ANM also turns off timer T9b.

Either party can terminate the connection by issuing a release (REL) message (turning on timer T1b), which is acknowledged with a release complete (RLC) message (turning off timer T1b). Upon receiving an RLC, an exchange (including any intermediate exchanges) must release the associated VPCI/VCI, the reserved bandwidth, and the associated OSID. Also, the process (the application entity instance) in each exchange, that supported this specific connection, is released.

THE B-ISUP ARCHITECTURE IN MORE DETAIL

The B-ISUP architecture is built around the Open Systems Interconnection (OSI) Model, as depicted in Figure 8–4.

The applications process (AP) is a set of capabilities within an open system that performs services on behalf of the end user (the application resting on top of the application layer). In B-ISUP, the term exchange application process describes all the application layer functions, and B-ISUP is part of the exchange application process.

In the OSI model, the APs use an application entity (AE) to communicate with each other. The AEs are invoked at run time to setup a connection between two or more APs. The B-ISUP AE provides all the capabilities needed at an exchange, and to simplify matters, only one single association object (SAO) and its single association control function (SACF) is contained in B-ISUP.

The SAO in the B-ISUP AE is classified as one of four application service elements (ASEs), which is the software that is invoked to perform B-ISUP functions. These ASEs are: (1) call control (CC), (2) bearer con-

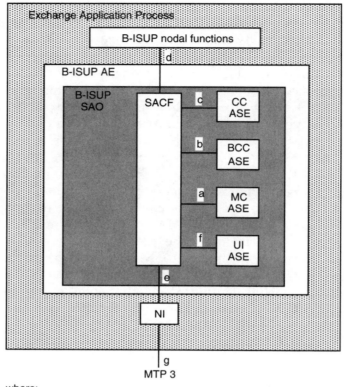

where:
AE   Application entity
ASE   Application service element
BCC   Bearer connection control
CC   Call control
MC   Maintenance control
NI   Network interface
SACF   Single association control function
SAO   Single association object
UI   Unrecognized information

Figure 8–4   The B-ISUP internal layer architecture.

nection control (BCC), (3) maintenance control (MC), and (4) unrecognized information (UI). We will have more to say about these ASEs shortly.

In the OSI Model, a unique and specific process is called an application process invocation, which starts an application entity invocation (AEI). An AE invocation is identified with an AEI identifier.

Each instance of the B-ISUP AE within each exchange is identified with a signaling identifier value (SID); it is allocated when the application entity invocation (AEI) is created and deallocated when the AEI is deleted. It is similar to the OSI service access point (SAP) or a UNIX socket.

Table 8–4 Mapping at the AP and ASE Interfaces

Interface (d) from AP	Interface (c) to CC ASE	Interface (b) to BCC ASE	Interface (a) to MC ASE
Set_Up req	Call_Set_Up req	Link_Set_Up req	
Address_Complete req	Call_Address_ Complete req	Link_Information req	
Incoming_Resources_ Accepted req		Link_Accepted req	
Incoming_Resources_ Rejected req		Link_Rejected req	Congestion_Level req
Release req/res	Call_Release req	Link_Release req/res	Congestion_Level req
Answer req	Call_Answer req	Link_Information req	
Progress req	Call_Progress req	Link_Information req	
Suspend req	Call_Suspend req		
Resume req	Call_Resume req		
Forward_Transfer req	Call_Forward_ Transfer req		
Segment req	Call_Segment req	Link_Information req	
Block_Resource req/res			Block req/res
Unblock_Resource req/res			Unblock req/res
Reset_Resource req/res			Reset req/res
User_Part_ Available req/res			User_Part_Test req/res
Check_Resource_ Begin req/res			Check_Begin req/res
Check_Resource_ End req/res			Check_End req/res
	Interface(f) to UI ASE		
Unrecognized_ Message_Type req	Unrecognized_ Message req		
Confusion req	Confusion req		

Table 8–5   Mapping of the Primitives and B-ISUP Messages

Interface (c) CC to ASE	Interface (b) to BCC ASE	Interface (a) to MC ASE	Message Type
Call_Set_Up req	Link_Set_Up req		Initial address
	Link_Accepted req		IAM Acknowledge
	Link_Accepted req	Congestion_Level req	IAM Reject
Call_Release req	Link_Release req	Congestion_Level req	Release
	Call_Release res		Release Complete
Call_Address_ Complete req	Link_Information req		Address Complete
Call_Answer req	Link_Information req		Answer
Call_Progress req	Link_Information req		Call Progress
Call_Suspend req			Suspend
Call_Resume req			Resume
Call_Forward_Transfer req			Forward transfer
Call_Segment req	Link_Information req		Segmentation

Figure 8–4 uses notations (a) to (g) to identify where primitives are exchanged between the B-ISUP entities. Primitives are valuable documentation tools that are used by designers to lay out the interfaces between the entities. The B-ISUP specification also provides guidance on how these primitives and their parameters are mapped into the messages that are transferred between exchanges.

Two tables help explain the overall architecture and relationships of the AP and ASEs and the relationships of the key primitives to B-ISUP messages. Table 8–4 provides a summary of the primitives invoked at interfaces (a) through (d) and (f). Table 8–5 shows the mapping relationship of these primitives to B-ISUP messages. Appendix 8B provides a description of all these and the other interfaces, their associated primitives, and the parameters associated with the primitives.

SUMMARY

B-ISUP and SS7 are partners in supporting the end users' connection. ATM's Q.2931 is a user-network interface (UNI) operating between the user device and the network node, and B-ISUP is a network-node interface (NNI) operating between the nodes within the network or between networks. B-ISUP is also employed as an internetworking interface allowing two networks to communicate with each other.

APPENDIX 8A: PARAMETERS USED IN B-ISUP MESSAGES

This appendix provides a summary of the parameters that are coded into the B-ISUP messages. The reader should study ANSI T1.648-1995 if more detailed information is needed. Also, several of these parameters are described in Chapter 7, and I refer you to that chapter where appropriate.

ATM adaptation layer (AAL) parameters: These parameters are described in Chapter 7. Be aware that although they have end-to-end significance, they are also processed by the users' local exchanges, but transferred transparently between local exchanges.

Access delivery information: Defined in ITU-T Recommendations only. It is coded in the address complete, answer, or release message to indicate if a setup message was or was not generated for this connection. (It usually is generated.)

Additional calling party number: Defined in ITU-T Recommendations only. It is used to provide an additional calling party number in case more than one party is involved in the initiation of a call.

Additional connected number: Defined in ITU-T Recommendations only. This parameter is present in an answer, initial address, or segmentation message if more than one connected number must be identified.

ATM cell rate: This parameter contains the cell rate (in number of cells per second) requested in the forward and backward directions for both cell loss priority = 0 and cell loss priority = 0 + 1.

Automatic congestion level: This parameter is sent to the exchange at the other end of a virtual path to indicate that a predefined level of congestion has occurred. Currently, congestion levels 1 and 2 can be coded in the field, but their meanings are not defined in B-ISUP, but left to specific implementations.

Backward narrowband interworking indicator: Since B-ISUP, ISUP and ISDN are far from being universal signaling protocols (dial-tone signaling will predominate for many years), this parameter is sent in the backwards direction to indicate that a non-ISDN node has been encountered within the network connection. It can also indicate if a non-SS7 node has been encountered.

Broadband bearer capability: This parameter is described in Chapter 7.

Broadband high layer information: This parameter is described in Chapter 7.

Broadband low layer information: This parameter is described in Chapter 7 and amplified with a field stating if the parameters are or are not in a prioritized order.

Call diversion information: Defined in ITU-T Recommendations only. See the next parameter.

Call diversion may occur: Defined in ITU-T Recommendations only. In the event a call is diverted (redirected), this parameter and the parameter above stipulates if the call can indeed be diverted and the reason for the diversion (user busy, mobile subscriber not available, etc.).

Call history information: This parameter is sent in the backward direction and contains information on the accumulated propagation delay encountered for this connection. The value is coded in binary form and represents ms.

Called party number: This parameter contains the identification of the called party. The address is coded as a 4-bit BCD digit for each value in the address. The actual numbering plan can vary and a field in this parameter identifies the type of numbering plan used in the message. With few exceptions, the ISDN telephony numbering plan is used (ITU-T Recommendation E.164). The parameter also contains a field called the "nature of address indicator," which provides the following information:

- Subscriber number
- Unknown (national use)
- National (significant) number
- International number
- Reserved for national use
- Subscriber number, operator requested
- National number, operator requested
- International number, operator requested
- No number present, operator requested
- No number present, cut-through call to barrier
- 950+ call from local exchange carrier public station, hotel/motel, or non-exchange access end office
- Test line test code
- Reserved for network specific use (no interpretation)

Called party subaddress: This parameter is described in Chapter 7.

Called party's indicators: This parameter is sent in the backwards direction and is used to indicate (1) if the called party is an ordinary subscriber or a pay phone, and (2) if the called party status is that of alerting or of no indication.

Calling party number: This parameter identifies the calling party and is coded with the same conventions as the called party number discussed earlier, except that the "nature of address" indicator may have slightly different values. The nature of address values are as follows:

- Subscriber number
- Unknown (national use)
- National (significant) number
- International number
- Reserved for national use
- Non-unique subscriber number
- Non-unique national (significant) number
- Non-unique international number

This parameter also contains fields to indicate if the calling party number is complete/incomplete, if it can be displayed or not, and if it is subject to screening.

Calling party subaddress: This parameter is described in Chapter 7.

Calling party's category: This parameter provides several types of information about the category of the calling party and (where operators must participate in the call) the service language that is to be spoken by the assistance operators. It provides the following additional information:

- Operator, language (French, English, German, Russian, Spanish)
- Reserved for administration's use
- Reserved for national use
- Ordinary calling subscriber
- Calling subscriber with priority
- Data call
- Test call
- Pay phone

Carrier identification code: This parameter is sent in the forward direction to identify the carrier selected by the calling party.

Carrier selection information: This parameter is used in conjunction with the carrier identification code to indicate if the transit network was selected by pre-prescription or by dialed input.

Cause indicators: This parameter is described in Chapter 7.

Charge indicator: This parameter is sent in the backward direction to indicate if the call is chargeable.

Charge number: If the call is chargeable, this parameter contains the number to which the call is to be charged.

Closed user group information: Defined in ITU-T Recommendations only. Closed user groups (CUGs) are used to filter access to a subscriber or a group of subscribers. They are also used to prevent someone from making a call on a facility.

Connected line identity request: Defined in ITU-T Recommendations only. This parameter is coded in the initial address message (IAM) to request the identity of the connected line.

Connected number: Defined in ITU-T Recommendations only. This parameter is used to identify the connected number.

Connected subaddress: Defined in ITU-T Recommendations only. This parameter is used for the same purpose as the connected number parameter.

Connection element identifier: This parameter is sent in the backwards direction to identify the ATM virtual connection. It contains the virtual path connection identifier (VPCI) and the virtual channel identifier (VCI). The VPCI represents a VPI on a given interface and is not the same as the value of the VPI in the ATM cell header in which the B-ISUP message resides. As stated in previous chapters, the VPCI is used instead of the VPI since virtual path cross-connects allow multiple interfaces to be controlled by a single signaling virtual channel. The values of VCI=5 and VPCI=0 are reserved for the signaling virtual channel.

Consistency check request information: This parameter is sent in the backward direction to provide information about the virtual circuit connection (the VPCI). It indicates if the VPCI check was successful, was not successful, or not performed.

Destination signaling identifier (DSID): This parameter identifies the call control association at the receiving end of the virtual circuit. It is used to correlate related messages to an ongoing call sequence.

Echo control information: This parameter is sent in the backward or forward direction to indicate if an echo control device is requested for the connection.

Egress service: This parameter is sent in the forward direction to provide network specific parameters associated with the terminating exchange.

Forward narrowband interworking indicator: This parameter is sent in the forward direction to indicate the signaling capabilities within the network connection when interworking with a N-ISDN unit has occurred. The fields indicate the following information:

- ISDN user part preferred all the way
- ISDN user part not required all the way

- ISDN user part required all the way
- Originating access non-ISDN
- Originating access ISDN
- ISDN user part not used all the way
- ISDN user part used all the way
- No interworking encountered
- Interworking encountered

Generic address: This parameter defines the type of address (such as dialed number, destination number, ITU-T spare, ASNI spare, etc.).

Generic digits: This parameter defines the type of digits; that is, how they are coded (examples: IA5, binary, BCD, etc.).

Generic name: This parameter defines whether a name can or cannot be presented to a party. If it is a calling name, this parameter indicates which one is it (i.e., original called name, redirecting name, or a connected name).

Inband information indicator: This parameter is sent in the backward direction to indicate that inband information is or is not available.

Jurisdiction information: This parameter is coded as an address.

Location number: Defined in ITU-T Recommendations only. This parameter is coded in the initial address message (IAM) to indicate: (1) if routing to a particular number is/is not allowed, (2) if the presentation of the number is allowed, (3) if screening of the number is provided. It also contains the number in question.

Maximum end-to-end transit delay: This parameter establishes the maximum acceptable transit delay for the call.

MLPP Precedence: This parameter (multilevel precedence and preemption) contains several fields and is sent in the forward direction to contain the following information:

- LFB allowed
- Path reserved
- LFB not allowed
- Flash override
- Flash
- Immediate
- Priority
- Routine

MLPP user information: This parameter is sent in the backward direction to identify that the called user is an MLPP user.

Narrowband bearer capability: This parameter is sent in the forward or backward direction to identify a requested or proposed N-ISDN bearer capability. This information is coded in the same form as the bearer capability information elements described in Q.2931 (see Chapter 7).

Narrowband high layer compatibility: This parameter is described in Chapter 7.

Narrowband low layer compatibility: This parameter is described in Chapter 7.

National/international call indicator: This parameter is coded to stipulate that the call is to be treated as a national or international call.

Notification: Defined in ITU-T Recommendations only. This parameter provides a wide variety of information about a call. Here are some examples:

- Other party added, disconnected, reattached
- Conference call is established, disconnected
- Call transfer
- Remote hold

OAM traffic descriptor: This parameter is coded in the same format as its counterpart in Q.2931 to indicate the number of cells per second for OAM traffic and whether traffic shaping is permitted.

Original called number: This parameter is sent in the forward direction when a call is redirected and it identifies the original call party. It is coded in the same format as the called party number described earlier.

Origination IC Point code: Defined in ITU-T Recommendations only. This parameter is simply the SS7 point code of the origination signaling point. It can be useful to determine where the call emanated (the MTP 3 label does not retain the origination point code).

Origination signaling identifier (OSID): The value in this parameter is assigned by the node initiating a call control or maintenance operation. It is used to identify the signaling association at the calling end.

Outgoing facility identifier: This parameter contains several fields and is sent in the backward direction to identify a facility selected at an outgoing gateway. It must contain a VPCI and an SS7 point code. The SS7 point code identifies the far-end switch.

Progress indicator: This parameter is sent in the forward or backward direction to describe any chosen event that has occurred during the lifetime of the connection. It contains the same information as its companion information element in Q.2931.

Propagation delay counter: This parameter is sent in the forward direction to provide information on the propagation delay encountered in the processing of a connection. The field is increased as the message is transferred through the network. The counter increments in integer multiples of 1 ms.

Redirecting number: This parameter is sent in the forward direction if a call is diverted and it indicates the number from which the call was diverted.

Redirection information: In the event that a call is diverted, this parameter contains information about the call rerouting or redirection. It yields the following information:

- Unknown/not available
- User busy (national use)
- No reply (national use)
- Unconditional (national use)
- No redirection (national use)
- Call rerouted (national use)
- Call rerouted, all redirection information presentation restricted (national use)
- Call diversion
- Call diversion, all redirection information presentation restricted
- Call rerouted, redirection number presentation restricted (national use)
- Call diversion, redirection number presentation restricted
- Deflection during alerting
- Deflection immediate response
- Mobile subscriber not reachable

Redirecting number: This parameter contains the number of the party that set up a redirection operation.

Redirection number: Defined in ITU-T Recommendations only. This parameter contains the number of the redirected number.

Redirection number restriction: Defined in ITU-T Recommendations only. This parameter stipulates if the redirected number can be presented to the called party.

Resource identifier: In the event resources in the network must be reset, blocked or unblocked, this parameter identifies those resources. It identifies if the source is (1) a local signaling identifier, (2) a remote signaling identifier, (3) a VPCI/VCI, or (4) a VPCI.

Segmentation indicator: This parameter is sent in the forward or backward direction to indicate if additional messages will or will not be sent pertaining to the full logical message.

Special processing request: This parameter is sent in the forward direction and specifies if the call requires special processing. The processing depends on the specific implementation in a B-ISUP network.

Suspend/resume indicators: As this name implies, this parameter is used in the B-ISUP suspend and resume messages to identify if the suspend or resume was initiated by the network or the network subscriber.

Transit network selection: This parameter is sent during the call setup to identify the transit network that is to be used to process the call.

User-network interaction indicator: This parameter is sent in the backward direction to indicate that the exchange is collecting more information from the calling party about the called party before proceeding further with the call.

User-to-user indicators: This parameter is sent in a request or a response to a request and provides user-to-user signaling supplementary services.

User-to-user information: This parameter is not processed by the interexchange network but is transferred transparently between the originating and terminating local exchanges.

APPENDIX 8B: B-ISUP INTERFACES, PRIMITIVES, AND PRIMITIVE PARAMETERS

This appendix provides a summary of the B-ISUP interfaces, primitives, and primitive parameters. The reader should study ANSI T1.648-1995 and ITU-T Q.2764 if more detailed information is needed.

The (a) interface is concerned with maintenance operations such as connection resets, blocking/unblocking, checking for resource availability, message compatibility checking, and so on. The primitives shown in Table 8B–1 are used to support these operations. The parameters used in the primitives are listed at the bottom of the table.

The (b) interface is concerned with setting up and clearing of connections between exchanges and is not concerned with user virtual connections. Table 8B–2 lists the primitives used for link management and their associated parameters. The table should be self-explanatory, if the reader has studied this chapter. Many of the parameters are mapped into the B-ISUP message information elements (explained in Appendix 8A.)

Table 8B–1   Primitives and Parameters at the (a) Interface

Primitive Name	Primitive Type and Associated Parameters			
	Request	Indication	Response	Confirm
Block	MCI/RI	MCI/RI	MCI	MCI
Unblock	MCI/RI	MCI/RI	MCI	MCI
Reset	MCI/RI	MCI/RI	MCI	MCI
User_Part_Test	MCI	MCI	MCI	MCI
Error	(1)	None	(1)	(1)
Congestion_Level	ACI	ACI	(1)	(1)
Check_Resource_Begin	MCI/RI	MCI/RI	MCI	MCI
Check_Resource_End	MCI	MCI	MCI/CCRI	MCI/CCRI

where:
MCI: Message compatibility information
RI: Resource identifier
ACL: Automatic congestion level
CCRI: Consistency check result information
(1):   Primitive not used
None: No parameter is contained in the primitive

Table 8B–2   Primitives and Parameters at the (b) Interface

Primitive Name	Primitive Contents for Associated Parameters													
	1	2	3	4	5	6	7	8	9	10	11	12	13	14
Link_Set_Up	QI	QI	QI		QI	QI	QI	QI	QI	QI	QI	QI	QI	
Link_Accepted	QI						QI							
Link_Rejected	QI													QI
Link_Information	QI	QI			QI	QI			QI		QI	QI	QI	
Link_Release	QIRC													QIRC
Link_Error														I

where:
QIRC: Stands for Request, Indication, Response, Confirmation, respectively and
1:     Message compatibility information   8:   Echo control information
2:     AAL parameters   9:   Maximum end-to-end transit delay
3:     ATM cell rate   10: Narrowband bearer capability
4:     Call history information   11: Narrowband low layer capability
5:     Broadband low layer information   12: OAM traffic descriptor
6:     Broadband bearer capability   13: Propagation delay counter
7:     Connection element identifier   14: Cause

Table 8B–3 Primitives and Parameters at the (c) Interface

Primitive Name	Primitive Contents for Associated Parameters																		
	1	2	3	4	5	6	7	8	9	10	11	12	13	14	15	16	17	18	19
Call_Set_Up	QI				QI	QI			QI	QI			QI	QI	QI	QI	QI		QI
Call_Address_Complete	QI	QI		QI				QI	QI		QI		QI			QI	QI		
Call_Release	QI							QI								QI	QI		
Call_Answer	QI	QI	QI					QI			QI		QI			QI	QI		
Call_Progress	QI	QI		QI				QI	QI		QI		QI			QI	QI		
Call_Suspend	QI																	QI	
Call_Resume	QI																	QI	
Call_Forward_Transfer	QI																		
Call_Exit																			
Call_Segment	QI		QI										QI			QI			
Call_Error								I											

where:

QIRC: Stands for Request, Indication, Response, Confirmation, respectively and

1: Message compatibility information
2: Backward narrowband interworking indicator
3: Broadband high layer information
4: Call history information
5: Called party indicators
6: Called party number
7: Calling party's category
8: Cause indicators
9: Charge indicator
10: Exchange type*
11: Forward narrowband interworking indicator
12: Inband information indicator
13: Narrowband high layer capability
14: National/international call indicator
15: Origination ISC point code
16: Progress indicator
17: Segmentation indicator
18: Suspend/resume indicators
19: Transit network selection

*The exchange type parameter is passed to the ASE so that the protocol can be varied depending on the role that the exchange is performing for this call/connection. Unlike the other parameters, it does not relate to a protocol information element.

Table 8B–4   Primitives and Parameters at the (d) Interface

Where following primitive is either M for mandatory, O for optional or — for not known for the related parameter in B-ISDN:

	PRIMITIVES			
	Request	Indication	Response	Confirm
1: Set_Up	X	X		
2: Address_Complete	X	X		
3: Incoming_Resources_Accepted	X	X		
4: Incoming_Resources_Rejected	X	X		
5: Release	X	X		
6: Release			X	X
7: Answer	X	X		
8: Progress	X	X		
9: Suspend	X	X		
10: Resume	X	X		
11: Forward_Transfer	X	X		
12: Segment	X	X		

Parameter Name	Primitive Contents for Associated Parameters											
	1	2	3	4	5	6	7	8	9	10	11	12
Message compatibility information	M	M	M	M	M	M	M	M	M	M	M	M
AAL parameters	O						O					
ATM cell rate	M											
Automatic congestion level				O	O			—				
Backward narrowband interworking indicator		M					—					
Broadband bearer capability	M											
Broadband low layer information	O						O				O	
Broadband high layer information	O										O	
Call history information							O					
Called party indicators		M						O				
Called party number	M											
Calling party's category	M											
Cause indicators		M		M	M	O		O				
Charge indicator		M					O	O				
Connection element identifier	O	O										
Echo control information	O	M										

(continued)

Table 8B–4   Continued

Parameter Name	Primitive Contents for Associated Parameters											
	1	2	3	4	5	6	7	8	9	10	11	12
Exchange type*	M											
Forward narrowband interworking indicator	—											
Inband information indicator		—					—	—				
Maximum end-to-end transit delay	O											
Narrowband bearer capability		—	—				—	—				
Narrowband bearer capability prime	—											
Narrowband high layer capability		—	—				—	—				O
Narrowband low layer capability	—							—				O
National/international call indicator	O											
OAM traffic descriptor	O						O					
Progress indicator	O	O			O		O	O				O
Propagation delay counter	M											
Segmentation indicator	O	O			O		O	O				
Suspend/resume indicators										M	M	
Transit network selection	O											

*The exchange type parameter is passed to the ASE so that the protocol can be varied depending on the role that the exchange is performing for this call/connection. Unlike the other parameters, it does not relate to a protocol information element.

The (c) and (d) interfaces are concerned with supporting a user's call. Most of the primitives in Tables 8B–3 and 8B–4 are mapped into corresponding B-ISUP messages and the parameters are mapped into the information elements of the messages. Once again, these tables are self-explanatory.

The primitives shown in Table 8B–5 pertain to the (e) interface and are concerned with the transfer of signaling units from SACF through its MTP 3 to another exchange.

The MTP_Transfer primitives are distributed to the connect AEIs based on the destination SID parameter according to the following rules (established in ANSI T1.648.4):

- If the Destination SID corresponds to an existing B-ISUP AEI, the message is distributed to that AEI.
- If the Destination SID does not correspond to an existing B-ISUP AEI, a new instance of B-ISUP, including an AEI, is created. This new instance is allocated with a new SID value.
- If the message does not contain a Destination SID parameter but

Table 8B–5   Primitives and Parameters at the (e) Interface

Primitive Name	Types			
	Request	*Indication*	*Response*	*Confirm*
1: Transfer	X	X		
2: Remote_Status		X		
3: Destination_Unavailable		X		
4> Destination_Available		X		

	Mappings			
	(g) from MTP 3	*(e) to SACF*	*(e) from SACF*	*(g) to MTP 3*
MTP_Transfer indication	X			
MTP_Status indication	X			
MTP_Pause indication	X			
MTP_Resume indication	X			
Transfer request			X	
MTP_Transfer request				X

Table 8B–6   Primitives and Parameters at the (f) Interface

Primitive Name	Types			
	Request	*Indication*	*Response*	*Confirm*
1: Unrecognized_Message	X	X		
2: Unrecognized_Parameter	X	X		
3: Confusion	X	X		

Parameter Name	Primitive Contents for Associated Parameters		
	1	2	3
Message compatibility information			M
Cause			M

it does contain an Origination SID parameter, a new instance of B-ISUP, including an AEI, is created. This new instance is allocated a new SID value.

The primitives shown in Table 8B–6 play a limited role dealing with the inability to recognize a message, a parameter in the message, or anything else (confusion) that cannot be processed.

Finally, interface (g) is concerned with the MTP 3/B-ISUP interface. This interface is described in the main body of this chapter (see Figure 8–1).

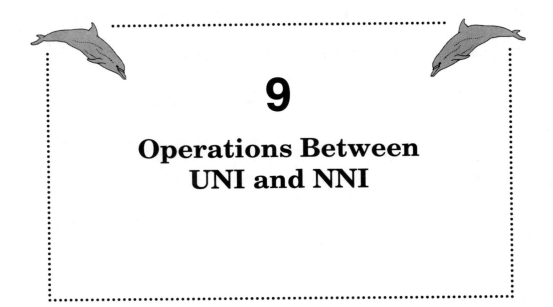

9

Operations Between
UNI and NNI

INTRODUCTION

This chapter pieces together the UNI and NNI operations and explains how the messages and parameters are interworked across these interfaces.

Due to the rather extensive analysis of the UNI and NNI operations in Chapters 7 and 8, respectively, I will not rehash timers or the details of the information elements in the messages. I will explain how the information elements in the messages correlate (map) to each other.

TYPICAL CALL SETUP AND RELEASE OPERATIONS

Figure 9–1 shows a typical call setup and release operation at both the UNI (with Q.2931) and NNI (with B-ISUP). User A initiates the connection by sending the Q.2931 SETUP message to its exchange (exchange A). At this switch, the Q.2931 message and its information elements are used to set up the virtual circuit and create the B-ISUP initial address message (IAM). After sending the CALL PROCEEDING message to user A, exchange A sends the IAM message through the network across intermediate exchanges (in this example, exchange B) to the terminating exchange (exchange C). The exchanges return IAAs upon receiving the IAM. At exchange C, the IAM is used to create the virtual circuit across the

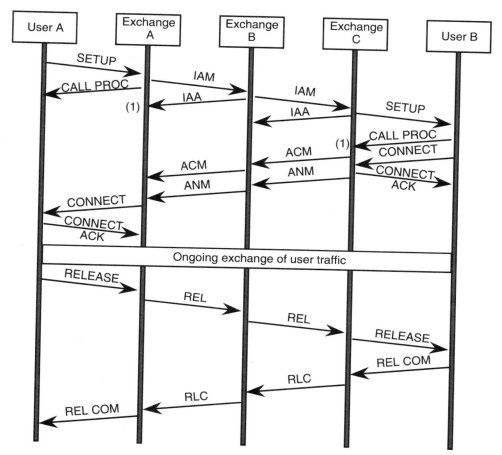

Note 1: Mapping of messages and information elements do not occur.

Figure 9–1   UNI and NNI operations.

UNI to user B by the issuance of the Q.2931 SETUP message, and user B returns the CALL PROCEEDING MESSAGE to its exchange.

If the user decides to accept the call, it sends an ALERT (optional) message and/or the CONNECT message. The ALERT message is mapped to the B-ISUP ACM and back to the Q.2931 ALERT at the originating UNI. The ALERT operations are not shown in this example, which uses the CALL PROCEEDING message instead.

The CONNECT is mapped to the B-ISUP and back to the Q.2931 CONNECT at the originating UNI. The CONNECT ACK messages acknowledge the CONNECT messages.

Table 9–1   SETUP ↔ IAM Mapping

SETUP Is Mapped to	IAM Is Mapped to	SETUP
AAL parameters	AAL parameters	AAL parameters
ATM traffic descriptor	ATM cell rate Additional ATM cell rate	ATM traffic descriptor

Broadband bearer
  capability
	Broadband bearer
	  capability
		Broadband bearer
		  capability

Broadband high layer
  information
	Broadband high layer
	  information
		Broadband high layer
		  information

Broadband sending complete	Not carried	No mapping
Called party number	Called party number AESA for called party	Called party number
Called party subaddress	Called party subaddress Calling party number AESA for calling party	Called party subaddress Calling party number
Calling party subaddress	Calling party subaddress	Calling party subaddress
Transit network selection	Transit network selection	
Quality of service	Quality of service	Quality of service

During these operations, the users and the exchanges are involved in creating each segment of the virtual circuit and allocating the resources that will be needed to support the call. After the successful completion of these operations, the users' exchange their traffic with each other.

In this example, user A initiates the release of the connection by sending a Q.2931 message to exchange A. The successful receipt of this message begins the disconnection of the virtual circuit and its associated resources by mapping the RELEASE message and its parameters into the B-ISUP REL, which is mapped back into the Q.2931 RELEASE message at the exchange C-user B UNI.

Table 9–2   CONNECT ↔ ANM Mapping

CONNECT Is Mapped to	ANM Is Mapped to	CONNECT
AAL parameters	AAL parameters	AAL parameters

Broadband low layer
  information
	Broadband low layer
	  information
		Broadband low layer
		  information

Table 9–3   RELEASE ↔ REL Mapping

RELEASE Is Mapped to	REL Is Mapped to	RELEASE
Cause	Cause indicators	Cause

The next section of this chapter describes the message mapping operations between Q.2931 and B-ISUP. For this example, it should be noted that the IAA message is not mapped to the CALL PROCEEDING message at the originating UNI (note 1 in Figure 9–1). Likewise, there is no mapping between CALL PROCEEDING and ACM at the terminating UNI.

MAPPING BETWEEN THE UNI AND NNI MESSAGES AND INFORMATION ELEMENTS

The mapping of the messages and information elements for the operations in Figure 9–1 are depicted in Tables 9–1 through 9–3. Table 9–1 shows the mapping of the SETUP and IAM, Table 9–2 shows the mapping of the CONNECT and ANM, and Table 9–3 shows the mapping of the RELEASE and REL messages.

Other mapping operations occur for other operations (i.e., ALERT). If you need more details of each mapping operation, I refer you to Bellcore GR-1417-CORE, Issue 2, November 1995. The ITU-T and ANSI specifications provide similar information.

SUMMARY

The protocols at the broadband UNI and NNI have been designed to interwork gracefully with each other. They are quite similar to each other, but different enough to warrant different specifications. Fortunately, the broadband signaling specifications provide mapping tables to define the relationships of the UNI/NNI messages and the information elements in the messages.

10

Other Broadband
Signaling Operations
and Performance Requirements

INTRODUCTION

This chapter examines other aspects of the UNI and NNI operations and how they are used in a Broadband Switching System (BSS). This term is introduced in this chapter due to its use by Bellcore. We will also examine some Bellcore specifications. Several configuration options are examined pertaining to the interworking of current systems and broadband signaling systems. In addition, point-to-multipoint calls are explained along with add services. The chapter concludes with an examination of performance requirements for a BSS.

CONFIGURATION OPTIONS

There are several ways that a BSS can be configured, and the decision on a configuration is left to the service provider. Figure 10–1 will be used during this discussion.

One approach, called an overlay, is shown in Figure 10–2. The existing CCS network is connected to the ATM-based network at ATM nodes through a CCS interface (CSS I/F), which acts as a gateway between the systems. B-ISUP messages conveyed between the BSS and the CCS SPs are provided by the MTP layers, which use the layer operation shown in Figure 10–1b. This approach is attractive because the BSS has access to

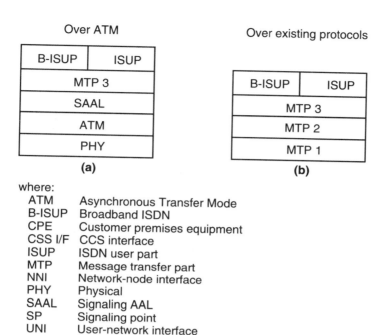

Over ATM | Over existing protocols

(a)

(b)

where:
ATM   Asynchronous Transfer Mode
B-ISUP   Broadband ISDN
CPE   Customer premises equipment
CSS I/F   CCS interface
ISUP   ISDN user part
MTP   Message transfer part
NNI   Network-node interface
PHY   Physical
SAAL   Signaling AAL
SP   Signaling point
UNI   User-network interface

Figure 10–1   Layers for configuration options.

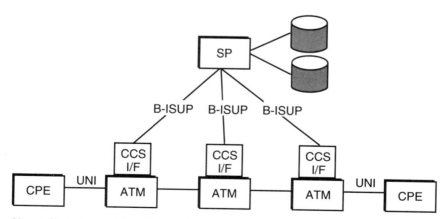

Note: Signaling point (SP) is typically a signaling transfer point (STP).

Figure 10–2   Overlay network, using B-ISUP with existing CCS network.

other resources (signaling points, databases) in the SS7 network. Therefore, this approach uses SCCP and TCAP for address translation and database access. The complexity arises because B-ISUP must be integrated into the signaling points, which forces the integration of the virtual circuit technology into the current physical circuit technology.

Another option is shown in Figure 10–3. In this situation, the CCS is not accessed. The BSSs are connected directly with ATM virtual channel connections over which the NNI signaling ATM adaptation layer (SAAL) is utilized. B-ISUP operates over SAAL to exchange messages between the BSSs. This approach uses the options shown in Figure 10–1a. It may be necessary to implement a subset of MTP 3 with this arrangement, because some of MTP 3 functions only come into play when messages are exchanged between STPs. With this approach, B-ISUP messages need only be exchanged between BSSs. But of course, it does not provide access to existing SS7 networks. I view this option as an interim measure, because it makes little sense to not draw on the resources of the current SS7 databases.

It is possible to use a hybrid configuration, as depicted in Figure 10–4. Both protocol stacks in Figure 10–1 are utilized. Access to the SS7 network is limited to one BSS hub. This configuration is attractive because it limits the number of links that connect the BSSs and the SPs, but it must be configured carefully due to the vulnerability of a single failure. As the BSS evolves and draws more heavily on the use of the SPs

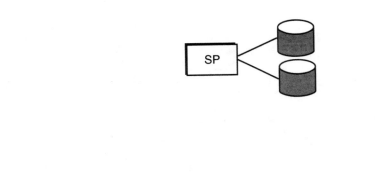

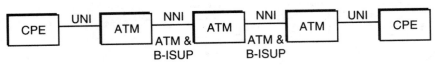

Figure 10–3   CCS network is not used.

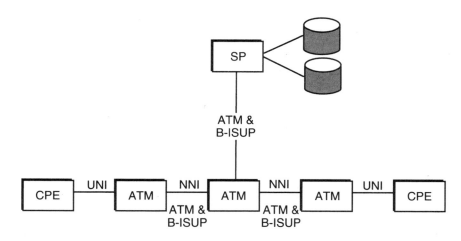

Figure 10–4   A hybrid configuration.

and databases, a fully meshed topology between the two systems is essential. A possible set of configurations is discussed next.

A likely configuration for the near future is shown in Figure 10–5. The ATM BSS machines (ATM BSS A, ATM BSS B, and ATM BSS C) interconnect through ATM virtual circuits. These machines are hooked up through signaling points (SPs), which are actually signaling transfer points (STPs) in this more detailed example.

This view represents one of Bellcore's approaches, which includes the signaling between two networks, labeled in Figure 10–5 as networks ABC and XYZ. This scenario would exist if a local exchange carrier (LEC) connected with an interexchange carrier (IXC).

This configuration is based on SS7 architecture and uses the quasi-associated signaling mode. An STP pair (STP A1, STP A2) is connected to another STP pair (STP B1, STP B2) in the other network through four D-link sets (known as a D-link quad[1]).

For this example, network ABC is the originating or terminating LEC network and network XYZ is the IXC network. The ATM BSS B is the gateway between the networks (the intermediate BSS).

Connections between the mated STPs are with C-links and connections between the ATM BSS machines are the STPs are with A-links.

---

[1]The SS7 links are explained in a companion book, *ISDN and SS7: Architectures for Digital Signaling Networks.*

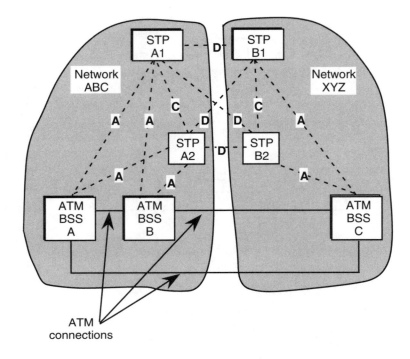

where: A = A links, C = C links, D = D links, and BSS = broadband switching system

Figure 10–5 Signaling network architecture.

POINT-TO-MULTIPOINT CALLS[2]

Because of the importance and wide use of telephone conference calls, multicasting data traffic, and video conferencing operations, broadband signaling networks have procedures to support these types of applications. The procedures are known as multicasting in most point-to-multipoint calls.

SIGNALING IDENTIFIERS (SIDs)

Thus far in this book, our discussions have concentrated on two identifiers: labels (VPIs, VCIs, VPCIs) and addresses (OSI, E.164, etc.).

---

[2]This example is derived from Bellcore GR-1431–CORE, Issue 2, November 1995. Some of the parameters and messages vary between Bellcore, ANSI, and ITU-T specifications.

Another identifier needs to be brought to our attention—the signaling identifier (SID), which is placed as a parameter in B-ISUP messages and used to identify a signaling association between a pair of BSSs.

The SIDs must remain constant for the life of the signaling connection and must be established for each BSS association. The SIDs are independently chosen and maintained by each BSS, and these BSSs may be in the same or different networks.

Figure 10–6 provides an example of how the SIDs are set up, used during the connection, and cleared. Exchange A selects SID = abc for the connection. This value is placed into the originating SID (OSID) parameter of the IAM and sent to exchange B. Upon receiving this message, exchange B selects SID = xyz for the connection and places this value in the OSID parameter of the IAA. Exchange B must also place SID = abc in the parameter of the IAA. Exchange destination SID (DSID) of the message to enable exchange A to correlate the two SIDs and the subsequent messages.

After the connection has been established, the two exchanges use the SIDs to identify all call control messages. These messages do not need to contain an OSID parameter; they contain the DSID of the recipient of the message. This rule holds true for the connection release messages, as well.

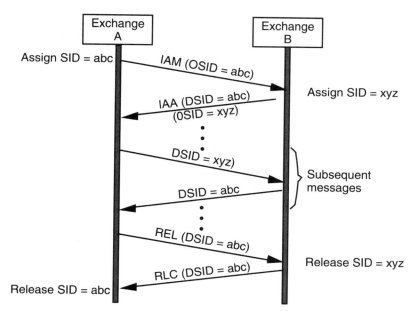

Figure 10–6   The SID operations.

Add Party Operations

This capability is implemented through the point-to-multipoint procedure as shown in Figure 10–7, which is an extension of Figure 7–10. This illustration shows the inclusion of three parties, but multiple parties may be connected with this operation.

The originating site issues a SETUP message across the UNI to the network. The network forwards this message to the destination in which the destination network node issues a SETUP across the UNI to the destination user.

The originating party (user A) is called the root party; this party is the source of the point-to-multipoint call. The destinations are called the

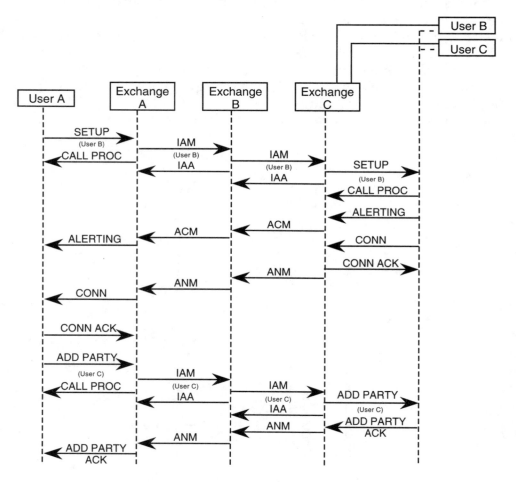

Figure 10–7   Point-to-multipoint operations.

leaf entries. It is the responsibility of the root to initiate the joining (adding) of all leaf entries to the call.

The originating exchange that receives the Q.2931 SETUP message determines if the call can be made and, if so, sends an IAM to the next (intermediate) exchange. The operations proceed in the ongoing manner discussed in Chapters 7 and 8. At the terminating exchange (exchange C), the B-ISUP messages are translated back to Q.2931 messages and vice versa between exchange C and user A.

Notice that an ALERTING message is sent in the backward direction (which is mapped into the B-ISUP ACM). The ALERTING message is optional; as explained in Chapter 7, it is not part of the ATM UNI specification (Version 3.1).

The addition of new leaf entries takes place from the root party through the use of the ADD PARTY message instead of the SETUP message. This message is invoked in Figure 10–7 to add party C to the connection.

The IAM for the call must contain the leaf party type parameter, and the origination connection link identifier parameter (containing the link identifier). In addition, the broadband bearer capability parameter must indicate in the user plane connection configuration field the "point-to-multipoint" operation. The other parameters that are required are ATM cell rate, quality of service, called party number, calling party's category, and origination signaling identifier.

For adding user C to this existing connection, the IAM must contain the destination connection link identifiers instead of the origination connection link identifier, and the connection element identifier parameter (VPCI/VCI).

PERFORMANCE REQUIREMENTS FOR THE SIGNALING VIRTUAL CHANNEL CONNECTION (VCC)

It was explained earlier that the VCI value of 5 is reserved for each virtual path connection (VPC) that is used for signaling. It is important that the signaling channel be provided with adequate bandwidth to support the broadband network. The various standards define the following requirements:

- At a minimum, the signaling systems shall support a peak cell rate of the signaling virtual channel ranging from $n \times 173$ cells/second (where $1 \leq n \leq 23$) and 4140 cells/second.

- As options, peak cell rates may be greater: (1) 5520 cells/second, (2) 8280 cells/second, or (3) 11040 cells/second.
- Cells transmitted through the signaling system must conform to a cell delay variation tolerance of 1000 μsec for peak cell rates below 4140 cells/second and 250 μsec for peak cell rate higher than 4140 cells/second.

These performance requirements are calculated on the 48 octets of the ATM cell and discount the AAL headers that reside in these 48 octets. (The network considers these 48 octets as user traffic). The peak cell rates contain "padding" to account for the overhead of OAM (operations, administration, and maintenance) cells that consume part of the channel bandwidth.

The values are inflated to reflect the OAM traffic. For example, a cell user payload (48 octets/cell) needs slightly over 166 cells/second (166.67) to support a 64 kbit/s application. But the figures cited above show that 173 cells/second are allocated to accommodate the OAM cells.

Table 10–1   PCR Values to Be Supported by Equivalent Bandwidth

PCR Value (cells/second)	Equivalent Bandwidth (bits/second)
0	0
152	56 kbit/s + OAM cells
$n \times 173$ where $n = 1, 2, ..., 23$	$n \times 64$ kbit/s + OAM cells
3,622	1.39 Mbit/s including OAM cells
$n \times 690$ where $n = 7, 8, 9, 10, 11, 13, 14, 15, 16,$ 17, 19, 20, 21, 22, 23, 25, 26, 27, 28, 29, 31, 32 33, 34, 35, 37, 38, 39, 40, 41, 42, 44, 45, 46, 47	Approximately $n \times 256$ kbit/s
$n \times 4,140$ where $n = 1, 2, ..., 23$	$n \times 1.544$ Mbit/s + OAM cells
$n \times 4,140$ where $n = 24, 25, ..., 85$	$n \times 1.544$ Mbit/s + OAM cells
96,111	36.86 Mbit/s including OAM cells
104,268	40.04 Mbit/s including OAM cells
$n \times 119,910$ where $n = 1, 2$	$n \times 44.763$ Mbit/s + OAM cells
353,207	135.63 Mbit/s including OAM cells

Note: Equivalent bandwidth entries for 56 kbit/s, $n \times$ DS0, $n \times$ DS1, and $n \times$ DS3 allow overhead for the Type 1 ATM Adaptation Layer (AAL) and OAM cells. The OAM cell overhead allows up to 1 OAM cell for every 128 User Information cells plus 1 cell/second for reporting Alarm Indicate Signal (AIS) and Far End Receive Failure (FERF) information.

Table 10–2   Cell Delay Variation Tolerance (CDVT) at the UNI

CDVT for DS1	CDVT for DS3	CDVT for STS-3c or STS-12c
—	—	50 microseconds
100 microseconds	100 microseconds	100 microseconds
150 microseconds	150 microseconds	150 microseconds
200 microseconds	200 microseconds	200 microseconds
250 microseconds	250 microseconds	250 microseconds
350 microseconds	350 microseconds	—
500 microseconds	500 microseconds	—

These figures also contain some extra padding to account for the varying use of AAL1 or AAL5 protocol data units, which consume different amounts (in the headers/trailers) of the 48 octet payload.

Bellcore provides some useful information (Bellcore GR-1110-CORE, Issue 1, September 1994) to correlate the ATM peak cell rate (PCR) to the required equivalent bandwidth. Table 10–1 is a summary of the PCR in cells/second and the equivalent bandwidth in bits/sec. Table 10–2 shows the amount of cell delay variation tolerance (CDVT) for user traffic in the ingress direction at the UNI (based on the two-point CDV definition in ITU-T Recommendation I.356). Table 10–3 correlates the sustainable cell rate (SCR) for VBR traffic to an equivalent bandwidth.

Table 10–3   Sustained Cell Rate (SCR) and Equivalent Bandwidth

SCR Value (cells/second)	Approximate Equivalent Bandwidth
0	0
152	56 kbps
$n \times 173$ where $n = 1, 2, ..., 23$	$n \times 64$ kbps
$n \times 690$ where $n = 7, 8, 9, 10, 11, 13,$ 14, 15, 16, 17, 19, 20, 21, 22, 23, 25, 26, 27, 28, 29, 31, 32, 33, 34, 35, 37, 38, 39, 40, 41, 43, 44, 45, 46, 47	Approximately $n \times 256$ kbps
$n \times 4,140$ where $n = 1, 2, ..., 85$	$n \times 1.544$ Mbps
$n \times 119,910$ where $n = 1, 2$	$n \times 44.736$ Mbps + OAM cells

SUMMARY

The evolution to an ATM-based broadband signaling network is underway. For the foreseeable future, overlay and hybrid networks will be prevalent.

As the broadband switching networks mature, more multimedia services will be created and the point-to-multipoint operations will become essential to the success of broadband signaling.

11

Private Network–Network Interface (PNNI)

INTRODUCTION

This chapter examines the Private Network–Network Interface (PNNI), a specification that is published by the ATM Forum. We learn the reason PNNI was developed as well as the PNNI operations. Two categories of PNNI protocols are described. One deals with route advertising and the other deals with signaling. The latter is the main focus of this chapter since this book concentrates on signaling protocols.

WHY ANOTHER NNI PROTOCOL?

One can reasonably ask why yet another set of specifications is required to define another protocol in the ATM environment. Indeed, for the ATM implementer or the user of the ATM equipment, the proliferation of new specifications creates more complexity in a network (the PNNI specification by itself is 365 pages in length). But PNNI is published for a very good reason. The ITU-T does not concern itself with the operations of private networks. (From the ITU-T perspective, the Internet is considered to be a private network.) Additionally, the ITU-T does not concern itself with the distribution of routing information, route discovery, or topology analysis. These operations have been left to the implementation of individual telecommunications administrations.

This approach is not the case with PNNI. The PNNI philosophy is that these important considerations cannot be left to individual implementations. For full interworking to occur between ATM-based networks and ATM switches, there must be standards in place to define how information is distributed between switches in an ATM network. Thus, PNNI consists of two major parts. The first part defines a protocol to exchange routing information for route discovery. It defines the operations for the distribution of topology and routing information between ATM switches. It allows the switches to compute paths through a network. The second part of PNNI is the focus on this book. It is used for signaling and defines the procedures to establish point-to-point or point-to-multipoint connections through an ATM network. In this regard, we will see that the PNNI signaling operations are quite similar to many of the other protocols described in this book because they are based on the Q.2931 specification.

OVERVIEW OF PNNI PROTOCOL

Figure 11–1 illustrates the reference model for PNNI. On the network side, it is divided into the three major areas of cell stream, NNI signaling, and the topology protocol. On the user side, it is divided into the cell stream, UNI signaling, and the management interface protocol. These operations are further divided into the components shown in the figure. The switching fabric is based on a cell technology switching elements. The call processing modules and signaling modules are based on

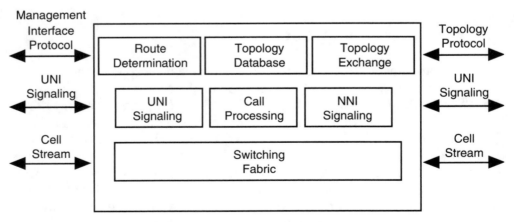

Figure 11–1   The PNNI reference model.

the Q Series specifications, and the topology exchange and route determination functions are based on shortest path route discovery technology.

Phase one of PNNI is designed to support all of the UNI release 3.1 capabilities and some of the UNI 4.0 capabilities. It is designed to support large networks, hierarchical routing, a wide variety of QOS, multiple routing metrics, source routed connection setups, and dynamic routing. In addition, it supports tunneling over virtual path connections (VPCs) and unicasting operations.

The signaling part of PNNI is derived from Q.2931 from which the ATM Forum's UNI signaling protocol was also derived. In this chapter, we will examine the unique aspects of the PNNI signaling protocol and refer to Q.2931 when appropriate. We will not revisit all the PNNI operations that use Q.2931 since this protocol was covered in Chapter 7.

I mentioned earlier that PNNI has two major aspects: that of signaling, which is the subject of this chapter, as well as that of route discovery, routing exchange, and topology analysis. For these latter operations, PNNI fills in the void left by the other signaling protocols published by the ITU-T, Bellcore, and ANSI. For those specifications, it is left to the vendor or designer to determine how these important operations are carried out. The ATM Forum has done a laudable job in forging this aspect of the PNNI to completion.

UNIQUE ASPECTS OF PNNI SIGNALING VIS-À-VIS Q.2931

Before we examine the PNNI signaling protocol, it will be useful to describe unique features not found in other signaling protocols described in this book. First, PNNI provides for a *crankback* operation. This allows for the release of the connection setup in progress when it encounters a failure at a node. The procedure allows the PNNI to perform alternate routing to find a nonblocked or better path through the network.

PNNI uses *link metrics* to determine a route. The link metric uses conventional shortest path first operations and may also employ Dykstra's algorithm to compute a spanning tree topology in the network. The link metric parameter requires that the values of the parameter for all links along a specific path be combined (summed) to determine whether the path is acceptable and/or optimal to carry the traffic to the destination address.

PNNI uses a *routing control channel*, which is a VCC employed for the exchange of PNNI routing protocol messages.

A *restricted transit node* is a node that can be used only under restricted and identified circumstances. It must always be an intermediate node in the call, because a restricted transit node is free to originate or terminate a call.

In addition, PNNI defines a *logical link* concept. Logical links exist between nodes in the network and can be a physical link or a VPC between two nodes. A logical link becomes operational when the attached nodes of the link initiate the exchange of information through a well known VCC, which we learned earlier is called the routing control channel (RCC). Logical link awareness is maintained through a procedure called the *Hello*, which stipulates the transmission of messages that are sent periodically between the two nodes to determine if the logical link is operational. These hello messages are exchanged between all intermediate neighbors to determine if all is well and the local state information of the neighbor nodes.

All the nodes in the PNNI network store *topology state parameters* (which are known as link state parameters in other route discovery protocols). This information is used in making routing decisions and also is used to accumulate the values to determine the shortest path based on the link metrics. Of course, certain types of topology state information such as delay and bandwidth may change. On the other hand, other information such as security may remain static. PNNI makes no distinction between dynamic or static parameters when it advertises routes between nodes.

PNNI SIGNALING SPECIFICATION MODEL

Figure 11–2 shows the topology and model for the PNNI interfaces. A calling user is called the *preceding side* and the called user is called the *succeeding side*. PNNI uses the same term, *forward direction,* as the other specifications in this book to connote the calling user to called user and the term *backward direction* to connote the called user to the calling user. In addition, the network that originates the call from the user is called the *preceding network* and the network that receives the call is called the *succeeding network*.

The PNNI model is further depicted in Figure 11–3, which is almost identical to the NNI signaling stack defined by other standards organizations. One difference pertains to the PNNI call control and PNNI protocol control. The call control layer services the upper layers for functions such as routing, routing exchange, and allocation of resources. The PNNI protocol control layer rests below the call control layer and thus provides services to call control. The PNNI call control layer is responsible for pro-

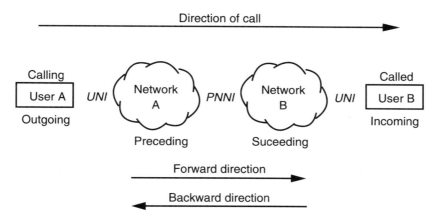

Figure 11–2 The PNNI interface and associated terms.

cessing the signaling. It operates with state machines for the incoming and outgoing calls. The layers below these two layers are based on the ITU-T Q.2xxx specifications described in earlier chapters in this book, and therefore, we shall not revisit those specifications here.

TERMS AND CONCEPTS

In order to grasp the basic concepts of how PNNI operates, we must first deal with several terms. In this section, I introduce the terms, and

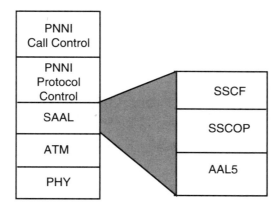

Figure 11–3 The PNNI control plane

then I explain them in more detail later in this chapter. Refer to Figure 11–4 during this discussion.

Figure 11–4 shows the PNNI hierarchy. It is so named because PNNI is designed for hierarchical routing. With this technique, nodes and their attached links at a given hierarchical level can be aggregated to a higher level, and this higher level can be once again aggregated into the next higher level.

This recursive aggregation is performed to (1) reduce the amount of routing information that is passed through a network, and (2) hide (if needed) topology information for privacy or security purposes.

At the lowest level in the hierarchy (shown in this figure as small black or white circles) is a relay node (an ATM switch, for example). These switches are connected by physical links (an OC-12 SONET link, for example). A collection of these switches form a hierarchy to the next higher level.

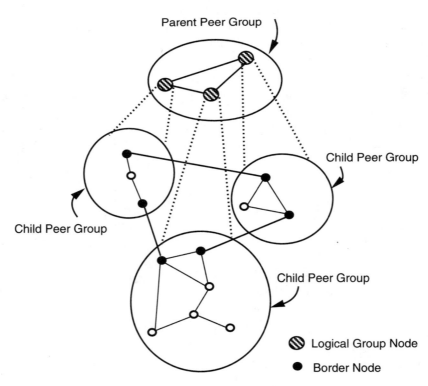

Figure 11–4   PNNI hierarchy.

The nodes at the same hierarchical level are known as a peer group. All nodes in a peer group exchange topology information with each other. As shown in this figure, a peer group may represent a lower-level peer group, or stated another way, lower peer groups can be aggregated to a higher peer group. The lower-level peer group is called a child peer group, and the upper-level group is called a parent peer group.

A group of nodes can be represented by one single node, which is called a logical node. Each child peer group is associated with (represented by) a logical group node inside the parent peer group. This relationship means that a logical group node represents a lower level peer group (the entire peer group). This relationship is depicted in this figure with the dashed lines.

Within the peer group, one logical group node is elected to be a peer group leader. This entity is responsible for route advertisements and topology aggregation for all the nodes in the peer group.

Another concept needs to be emphasized. The logical node is an abstract representation of a group of physical nodes. Therefore, the aggregated topology information associated with this logical node is actually a representation of the connectivity of the physical nodes.

The figure also shows the border node (black circles). This node is so defined if it has at least one attachment to another peer group. No restriction is placed on how many border nodes are configured in a PNNI network.

PNNI METRICS

Modern routing technology is based on a number of criteria called type of service factors (TOS), an Internet term for quality of service factors (QOS). These factors are defined by the network administrators and users and may include criteria such as delay, throughput, or security needs. The path through an internet is chosen based on the ability of the routers and networks to meet a required service.

This technique is also called link state routing, because the TOS values are applied to each communication link in the internet. A link metric is defined as the sum of a link state parameters (based on TOS) along a given path from a source address to a destination address. One of the purposes of PNNI is to provide means to advertise these metrics in order for a node to choose a "best" path (known as the shortest path) between two nodes. The length of the shortest path between the nodes is known as the distance between the nodes.

In typical large networks, there will be more than one path available from one node to another. Moreover, the various combinations of paths in a network may make the advertisements of all possibilities an onerous task. However, if a node in the network (say, a PNNI logical group node) somehow aggregates these many metrics to a shorter summary, and then advertises this summary, the task becomes feasible.

However, metric aggregation has a price to pay for this usefulness. In many situations, it will not lead to the optimum route. In these systems, one must weigh the amount of aggregation versus the accuracy of the aggregation.

To illustrate this point, consider Figure 11–5, which is extracted from the topology from the previous figure. Four nodes are connected to each other with four physical links. I change the topology in the bottom part of the figure to a meshed topology to make some points regarding metric aggregation. Nodes A, B, C, and D are now fully connected with

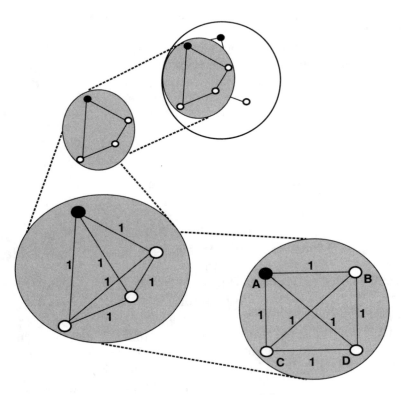

Figure 11–5   Link metrics.

six links.[1] Link state parameters of 1 are assigned to each link for this simple example.

Metric Aggregation

The metrics for the fully meshed 6-link network in Figure 11–6a, (the original graph) are aggregated to a 5-link network (Figure 11–6b, which is a subgraph). The dashed lines in the Figure 11–6 indicate that links have been eliminated from the network logical topology. Stated another way, they have been aggregated out of the graph.

A key goal in metric aggregation is to create a fully connected subgraph that has small stretch factor. The stretch factor is the maximum ratio of the distance in the subgraph to the distance in the original graph. For the 5-link subgraph, the stretch factor is 2, and five links are used to maintain the logical full-mesh topology. The compromise from the original graph is that the distance between B and C is now 2, but the aggregation translates to fewer variables in an advertisement. Furthermore, due to costs, it may be preferable to not have a physical link between B and C. Let's assume the links are T1 channels, for example. These links are expensive to lease, and the nature and amount of traffic between B and C may not warrant the cost of the T1 link.

To continue this example, Figure 11–6c shows another possibility for aggregating the metrics for this network. The 3-link aggregation still provides full connectivity, with the stretch factor remaining at 2. The compromise is that the distances between nodes A–C and B–C is now 2. Once again, this compromise may or may not be desirable, depending upon the nature of traffic between these nodes and the costs to provide direct links between them.

PNNI does not tell the network manager how to make the decisions on the physical topology, but it does provide a tool for advertising the topology and for using the network effectively.

---

[1]This analysis is based on several papers on the subject. I recommend for the reader who wishes more details: (1) David Peleg and Alejandro A. Schaffer, "Graph Spanners," *Journal of Graph Theory*, 13 (1), 1989. (2) Numerous ATM Forum working papers. See ATM Forum Contributions 94-0606, 95-0153, 94-0449. (3) Whay C. Lee (whay@prospero.dev.cdx.mot.com) is a noted expert in this field, and any of his papers are recommended. Mr. Lee contributed to most of the ATM papers, and (4) Whay C. Lee, "Topology Aggregation for Hierarchical Routing in ATM Networks," *Computer Communication Review*, 25 (2) April, 1995.

(a) Fully meshed nodes:

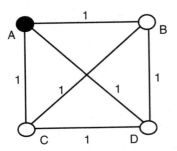

(b) Logically meshed with five links and stretch factor = 2:

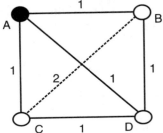

(c) Logically meshed with two links and stretch factor = 2:

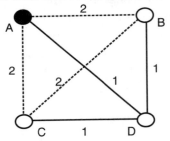

Figure 11–6   Metric aggregation.

In ATM networks, it is likely that the link attributes may vary from node to node. Even if the links are the same (for example, all OC-12 links), their utilization may vary, with some links carrying more traffic than others. This situation gives rise to different TOS values with regard to delay and throughput.

Figure 11–7 shows examples of metric aggregation with varying link attributes. Figure 11–7a shows a fully meshed network; Figure 11–7b shows a 5-link aggregation; and Figure 11–7c represents a minimum spanning tree with a 3-link aggregation.

This example illustrates that shorter paths may be available between physically adjacent nodes through nonadjacent nodes. The direct physical path between nodes A and C is 4, yet the aggregated path distance between A and C through B is 3. This situation can occur if, as examples, (1) node A's link to C is congested, (2) the link is operating at a low bit-rate, (3) the metric represents a high cost in relation to the error rate on the link, and so on.

Routing exchange information is advertised in a PNNI system by each node flooding PNNI topology state elements (PTSEs) within a desig-

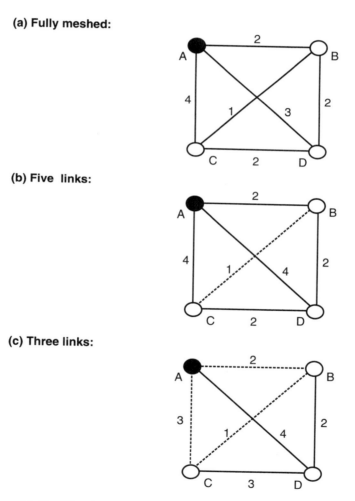

Figure 11–7   Metric aggregation with varying link attributes.

nated part of the overall network, which is called a peer group (see Figure 11–8). The information includes the node identity and the status of its links to its neighbors.

This information is used to keep a topology database updated at each node in the peer group. In effect, the topology database is a reflection of the information in the PTSEs and contains all the needed information to calculate a route from any node in the peer group to any other node. The PTSEs contain link state parameters (also called topology state parameters) and nodal state parameters. The former describes the state of each link at a node; the latter describes the state and characteristics of the node.

Topology state parameters are classified as follows (and they may be static or dynamic; PNNI does not care):

- *Attribute:* A single value, considered individually when making a routing decision (for example, link failure attribute that causes a link not to be selected for a route)
- *Metric:* An accumulation of values along a path (for example, a delay metric on each link that is added up for the end-to-end path.

The PTSEs are transmitted in a PNNI topology state packet (PTSP) and they must be acknowledged by the receiving node. Upon receiving a PTSP, a node examines it and performs the following actions:

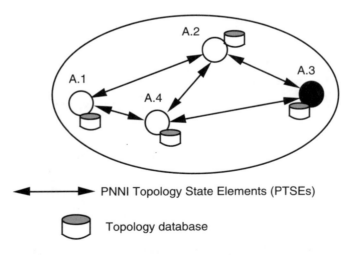

Figure 11–8   Exchanging information within a peer group (PG).

- If the PTSE is new or more recent than the current copy that is in the topology database, it is placed in the database.
- This PTSE is sent out on all the node's links except the link from which the information was received.

These operations are an ongoing activity, and a PTSE is sent whenever something changes, or on a periodic basis. At the topology database, entries are removed if they are not refreshed within a specific period. A node can only resend a PTSE that it originated.

HORIZONTAL AND OUTSIDE LINKS

Between lowest level nodes, connections are made by "logical links," which are either physical links or virtual path connections (VPCs) (see Figure 11–9). Links between two lowest level nodes in the same peer group cannot be aggregated. For example, if two physical links connect a pair of lowest level nodes, they are represented by two separate logical links. Two terms are important in this discussion: logical links inside a peer group are called horizontal links and logical links that connect two peer groups are called outside links.

When a logical link is set up and becomes operational, the neighbor nodes exchange information though a well-known VCC. This VCC is

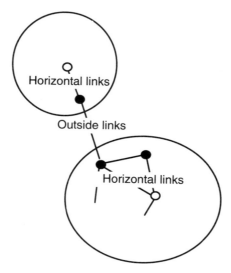

Figure 11–9   Horizontal links and outside links.

called a PNNI routing control channel (RCC). As we shall see later, a special protocol called the *Hello* protocol sends *Hello* packets across the RCC to keep neighbor nodes aware of each other's existence and the state of their communications channels. We shall also see that the PNNI *Hello* protocol allows a node to determine if it belongs to a peer group or not.

PNNI HIERARCHY EXAMPLE

As we just learned, the PNNI architecture is based on a hierarchical structure. Nodes are associated with level in a hierarchy and nodes that belong to the same hierarchy are in the same peer group. An example of the PNNI hierarchy, which I have derived from the ATM Forum PNNI specification, is provided in Figure 11–10. The numbers and alphanumerics in this figure represent addresses. They are drawn in place of specific addresses for ease of explanation. The highest hierarchy of this figure is peer group A, identified with the address of A. The nodes inside the group are identified as A1, A4, and so on. Within each peer group, there is a peer group leader whose responsibility is to receive topology information from all nodes in the group and advertise this information to other groups. The information that is advertised is "filtered" in that summary information is given to the other groups.

The next level of the PNNI hierarchy is shown with peer groups A.1, A.2, and so on. Within these peer groups are other nodes labeled as A.1.3, A.4.1, and so on. PNNI establishes rules about how messages can be sent up and down the hierarchy based on the functions of the nodes in a peer group. Once again, this concept is to place restrictions on how many route advertisements can be sent between nodes.

A logical group node represents a peer group in the next PNNI routing hierarchy. In Figure 11–10, logical group node A.2 represents peer group A.2 in the next higher level of the hierarchy, in this case, peer group A (PG (A)).

The functions and characteristics of the logical group node are as follows (and see Figure 11–11):

* Aggregates and summarizes information about its child peer group
* Floods this information to its own peer group

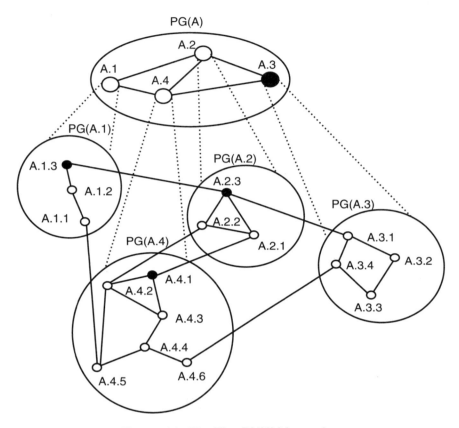

Figure 11-10 The PNNI hierarchy.

- Passes information about its peer group to the peer group leader (PGL) of the child peer group (this PGL floods this information within the peer group)
- Does not participate in the signaling operations
- The functions that define—for example, PGL A—are located in node A.2, which is implemented in a physical switching system (e.g., an ATM switch) containing the lowest level node (for example, A.2.3)
- Any node can become a peer group leader (if it is so configured)

The information flow up to the peer group leader is reachability, which contains summarized address information that is used to decide

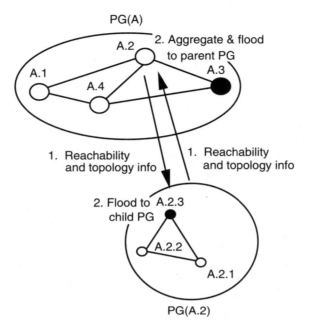

Figure 11–11   PNNI information exchange.

which addresses can be reached through the lower level peer group, and topology aggregation, which is summarized topology information that is used to route in and across the peer group.

The purpose of topology aggregation is to reduce the amount of information that is exchanged between nodes (or nodes between networks) about routes between nodes. The aggregation of routing information reduces the overhead in the network or networks by eliminating or decreasing the amount of information that must be exchanged to determine an efficient route between two endpoints.

Topology aggregation is also used to hide the details of a specific topology from another node that, for example, has no need to know about the minutiae of each individual route in the node's network. This aspect of topology aggregation may stem from security/privacy considerations, or the well-founded design principle of keeping network-specific operations within that network.

Whatever the rationale may be for link aggregation, Figure 11–12 shows the ideas behind it. In peer group A, noted as PG(A), the link between A.2 and A.4 is a logical link, because two physical links connect A.2 and A.4. They are the links between (1) A.2.2 and A.4.2, and (2) A.2.2 and A.4.1.

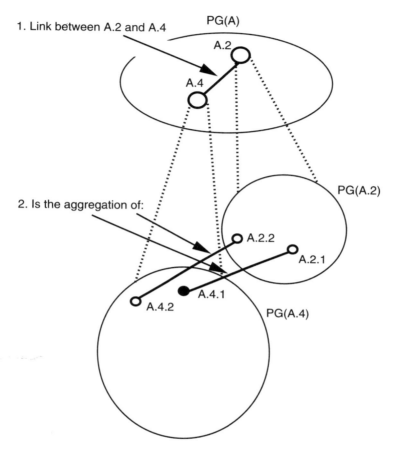

Figure 11–12   Link aggregation.

PNNI SIGNALING MESSAGES

The basic messages for PNNI signaling are derived from Q.2931. Table 11–1 lists these messages and their major functions. You can refer to earlier chapters for a detailed description of these messages. My intent in this section is to describe parameters in the messages that are unique to PNNI that are not defined in the other signaling specifications in this book.

A Look at the SETUP Message Information Elements

In this section we examine the SETUP message information elements that are unique to PNNI and not found in the other specifications.

**Table 11–1   The PNNI Messages for Call and Connection Control
(Point-to-Point)**

Message	Function
Call establishment	
SETUP	Initiate the call establishment
CALL PROCEEDING	Call establishment has begun
CONNECT	Call has been accepted
ALERTING	Called party has been alerted
Call clearing	
RELEASE	Initiate call clearing
RELEASE COMPLETE	Call has been cleared
Miscellaneous	
STATUS ENQUIRY (SE)	Sent to solicit a status message
STATUS (S)	Sent in response to SE or to report error
NOTIFY	Sent to provide additional information about a call

Calling Party Soft (permanent virtual path connection [PVPC] or permanent virtual channel connection [PVCC]). This information element indicates the VPI or VPI/VCI values used for the PVC segment for the calling connecting point. If no VPCs are configured for the use of logical links on a physical interface, a signaling channel designated as VPI = 0 controls all the virtual paths on the interface. Multiple virtual path connections (VPCs) are supported by PNNI to multiple destinations through a single physical interface. In this configuration, each VPC that is configured for use as a logical link must have a signaling channel associated with it. The virtual channels of these VPCs are controlled by the associated signaling pertaining to that particular VPC. This means that the signaling channel (which is the default channel of VPI = 0) on the same physical interface does not control the virtual channels that are used as logical links within PVCs. However, this default signaling channel does control all the remaining virtual channels and virtual paths on the physical link.

Called Party Soft (PVPC or PVCC). This information element indicates the VPI or VPI/VCI values of the PVC segment between the called connecting point and the user of a PVPC or PVCC, respectively.

Available Bit Rate (ABR) Parameters. The values in this information element pertain to the ABR class of service that is defined by the

ATM Forum in its UNI specification. This class of service was established by the ATM Forum because the ITU-T basic documentation did not provide for this feature.

In accordance with ATM Forum UNI 4.4, the parameter defaulting for the ABR parameters is performed by the network side of the calling user UNI. In the case of a soft PVPC or PVCC setup, it is the responsibility of the originating switch to send the setup message containing the ABR parameters. PNNI permits the ABR parameters to be adjusted by each switching system in the PNNI network hierarchy. This feature allows a network to protect resources or to modify the request so that the resources can meet the ABR parameters.

PNNI Available Bit Rate (ABR) Descriptors

Parameter values in each direction can be negotiated by either side for peak cell rate (PCR), initial cell rate (ICR), transit buffer exposure (TBE), rate increase factor (RIF), and rate decrease factor (RDF). If the network node is able to provide the requested PCR and ABR parameter values, the node must progress the call towards the called user with the original parameters. If it is not able to provide the requested PCR, but it is able to provide at least MCR value, then the node shall also progress the call towards the called user after it adjusts the PCR value to what it can handle. The adjusted PCR value must be greater or equal to MCR.

The PNNI node is allowed, if required, to also adjust either in the forward or backward directions the ABR setup parameters, ABR initial cell rate, ABR transfer buffer exposure, rate increase factor and rate decrease factor. Table 11–2 summarizes the changes that can be made by a PNNI node.

The succeeding side must adjust the accumulative RM fixed round-trip parameter within the ABR information element. The adjustment amount is the sum of the forward and reverse direction fixed portion of

Table 11–2 Permissible Modifications

Parameter for a Given Direction	Modification by the Network
PCR	Decrease only
ICR	Decrease only
TBE	Decrease only
RIF	Decrease only
RDF	Increase only

the RM cell relay including forward and reverse link propagation delays and any fixed processing delays that would be encountered within each PNNI switching system. The adjustment value is added to the cumulative RN fixed round trip-time parameter.

The cumulative RM fixed round-trip parameter will be adjusted in the first and last switching systems of full call path of the network side of the UNI. Once again, the amount of the adjustment is the sum of the forward and reverse direction fixed portion of the RM cell delay at the UNI. Additionally, it includes the forward and reverse link propagation delays up to network boundary and fixed processing delays at the UNI.

DESIGNATED TRANSIT LIST (DTL)

The designated transit list includes the logical nodes (and perhaps logical links) that a connection traverses through a peer group at some level of a PNNI hierarchy. The DTL list is coded in the SETUP and ADD PARTY messages within a designated transit list information elements. When the DTL is processed in each node in the path, the node determines whether any DTLs need to be added to the DTL stack (a stack is a representation of the hierarchically complete source route with the last-in/first-out list of DTLs). During this determination, the PNNI node determines whether any DTLs need to be removed from the stack and then processes the remaining stack to prepare it for transmission to the next node.

With regard to the crankback, if the call cannot be forwarded within a PNNI domain, then it can be cranked back. If the call goes all the way to the called user and gets rejected, this is not a crankback. In such cases the RELEASE or RELEASE COMPLETE message is sent by the called user. Crankback is used when reachability cannot be obtained, resource problems occur, or an error in DTL processing occurs. It is also possible for a crankback to occur because the path selection of sum nodes determines that no paths meet the quality constraints for the connection.

Crankbacks may result in alternate routing being attempted. But, this is an implementation decision based on the network. Crank back may also crank back to the next level in a PNNI hierarchy.

SOFT PERMANENT VIRTUAL CONNECTION PROCEDURES

Two network interfaces that serve the permanent virtual connection will establish and release a soft PVPC/PVCC. The influence of this connection are identified by assigning unique ATM addresses, which must include the SEL octet in the ATM address field.

One of the network interface endpoints owns the PVPC/PVCC and, therefore, assumes the responsibility for establishing and releasing the connection. This interface is called the calling endpoint. In order to establish a PVPC/PVCC, the endpoints must be identified. The calling endpoint is identified in the calling party number information element and the network management system provides the ATM addresses of the endpoints for the connection as well as the necessary information about the VPI/VCI that are used at the two endpoints.

It is important to note that parameters of the PVPC or PVCC are established administratively. They are separate from a process that establishes the soft PVPC/PVCC. Therefore, negotiation of these end-to-end parameters is not permitted.

Crank back

As we discussed earlier in this chapter, the crankback information element indicates that crankback procedures have been initiated. The information element also identifies the node or link where the connection could not be accepted. It also contains an identifier to note the level within the PNNI hierarchy at which crankback is being executed.

INFORMATION ELEMENTS FOR THE SUPPORT OF OTHER SERVICES

PNNI defines the support of other services, such as 64 kbit/s-based circuit mode services. These capabilities and information elements have been described in the material in this book dealing with Q.2931.

SUMMARY

The private network–network interface performs two major services in the broadband network. First, it provides a protocol for route advertising and guidance on link aggregation procedures. Second, it defines the signaling operations that are to be imployed in a private network based on Q.2931.

PNNI should play a valuable role in broadband networks since, heretofore, there has been no specification defining how routing exchange information is to be exchanged between switches. PNNI has not yet seen implementation in commercial systems since it is a relatively new specification.

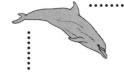

Abbreviations

AAL CP: AAL common part
AAL5: ATM adaptation layer, type 5
ACL: Automatic congestion level
AESA: ATM end system address
ARP: Address Resolution Protocol
AA: Administrative authority
AAL: ATM adaptation layer
ACCS: Automated calling card service
ACM: Address complete message
AE: Application entity
AEI: Application entity invocation
AFI: Authority format identifier
AIS: Alarm indicate signal
AP: Applications process
ASE: Application service element
ATM: Asynchronous Transfer Mode
B-ISDN: Broadband-ISDN
B-ISUP: Broadband-ISDN user part
BC: Bearer capability
BCC: Bearer connection control
BER: Basic encoding rules
BGAK: Begin acknowledge
BGN: Begin
BGRE: Begin reject
BOM: Beginning of message
BR: Buffer release
BRI: Basic rate interface

BSS: Broadband Switching System
C: Cell loss priority
CAC: Connection admission control
CBR: Constant bit rate
CC: Call control
CC: Country code
CCIS: Common channel interoffice signaling
CCRI: Consistency check result information
CCITT: International Telecommunications Union-Telecommunication Standardization Sector (see also ITU-T)
CCS: Common channel signaling
CCS I/F: CCS interface
CMIP: Common management information protocol
COM: Continuation of message
CPCS: Common part convergence sublayer
CPCS: Common part CS
CPCS-UU: Common part convergence sublayer-user-to-user
CPE: Customer premises equipment
CPI: Common part id
CPI: Common part indicator
CRC: Cyclic redundancy check
CS: Convergence sublayer

CUG: Closed user group
DCC: Data country code
DFI: Domain specific part identifier
DN: Destination network
DPC: Destination point code
DSAP: Destination SAP
DSID: Destination signaling identifier
DSP: Domain specific part
DSS: Digital subscriber signaling system
ENDAK: End acknowledge
E800: Enhanced 800
EOM: End of message
ER: Error recovery
ERAK: Error recovery acknowledge
ESI: End system identifier
FEC: Forward error correction
FERF: Far End Receive Failure
FOT: Forward transfer message
GFC: Generic flow control
GSM: Global systems for mobile communications
GT: Global title
HEC: Header error check
HEC: Header error control
HO DSP: High order domain specific part
IAA: IAM acknowledgment
IAM: Initial address
IC: Interchange carrier
ICD: International code designator
ICI: Intercarrier interface
ID: Interface data
id: Identification
IDI: Initial domain identifier
IDP: Initial domain part
IE: Information elements
IP: Internet Protocol
IPI: Initial protocol identifier
ISDN: Integrated Services Digital Network
ISUP: ISDN user part
IT: Information type
ITU-T: International Telecommunications Union-Telecommunication Standardization Sector (ITU-T, formerly, the CCITT)
IXC: Interchange carrier
LCN: Logical channel number
LE: List element
LEC: Local exchange carrier
LI: Length indicator

LLC: Low layer compatibility
LM: Layer management
LMI: Local management interface
MC: Maintenance control
MCI: Message compatibility information
MD: Management data
MID: Message id
MTP 3: Message transfer part 3
MTP: Message transfer part
MU: Message unit
MUSN: MU sequence number
N-BC: Narrowband bearer capability
N-HLC: Narrowband high layer capability
N-ISDN: Narrowband Integrated Services Digital Network
N-LLC: Narrowband low layer compatibility
NDC: National destination code
NNI: Network-node interface
NNI: Network-to-network interface
NSAP: Network service access point
N(S)N: National (significant) number
OSI Model: Open Systems Interconnection Model
OAM: Operations, administration, and maintenance
OUI: Organization unique ID
OPC: Originating point code
OSID: Origination signaling identifier
PAD: Padding
PBX: Private branch exchange
PC: Point code
PCI: Protocol control information
PCM: Pulse code modulation
PCR: Peak cell rate
PCS: Personal communications services
PDU: Protocol data unit
PHY: Physical layer
PID: Protocol id
PL: Physical layer
PM: Physical medium sublayer
PRI: Primary rate interface
PTI: Payload type identifier
PTO: Public telecommunications operators
PVC: Permanent virtual circuit
QOS: Quality of service
REL: Release
RES: Resume
RJE: Remote job entry

RLC: Release complete
ROSE: Remote operations service element
SAAL: Signaling ATM adaptation layer
SACF: Single association control function
SAO: Single association object
SAP: Service access point
SAR: Segmentation and reassembly
SCCP: Signaling connection control point
SCP: Service control point
SD: Sequenced data
SDU: Service data unit
SE: Status enquiry
SEL: Selector
SID: Signaling identifier
SIO: Service information octet
SLS: Signaling link selection code
SN: Sequence number
SN: Subscribers number
SNAP: Subnetwork access protocol
SNMP: Simple Network Management Protocol
SNP: Sequence number protection
SONET: Synchronous Optical Network
SP: Signaling point
SPF: Shortest path first
SPI: Subsequent protocol identifier
SS7: Signaling System Number 7
SSAP: Source service access point
SSCF: Service-specific coordination function
SSCOP: Service-specific connection-oriented protocol
SSCOP-UU: SSCOP user-to-user

SSCS LM: Service specific convergence sublayer layer management
SSCS: Service specific convergence sublayer
SSM: Single segment message
SSN: Subsystem number
SSP: Service switching point
STAT: Solicited status response
STP: Signaling transfer point
SUS: Suspend message
SVC: Switched virtual call or channel
TA: Terminal adapter
TCAP: Transaction capabilities application part
TC: Transmission convergence sublayer
TC: Trunk code
TCP/IP: Internet Protocols
TDM: Time division multiplexing
TUP: Telephone user part
UD: Unnumbered data
UI: Unrecognized information
ULP: Upper layer protocol
UNI: User-network interface
USTAT: Unsolicited status
VBR: Variable bit rate
VC: Virtual channel
VCC: Virtual channel connection
VCI: Virtual channel identifier
VCI: Virtual circuit identifier
VPC: Virtual path connection
VPCI: Virtual path connection identifier
VPI: Virtual path identifier
VPN: Virtual private network

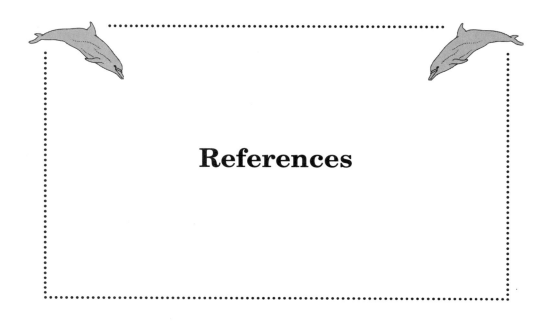

References

In addition to the formal standards for the systems described in this book, these references should prove useful to the reader. Many of them were used for the development of this material.

[AHMA93] Amhad, R., and Halsall, F. (1993). Interconnecting high-speed LANs and backbones, *IEEE Network*, September.

[AMOS79] Amos, J.E., Jr. (1979). Circuit switching: Unique architecture and applications. *IEEE Computer*, June.

[ARMT93] Armitage, G.J., and Adams, K.M.(1993). Packet reassembly during cell loss, *IEEE Network*, September.

[ATM92a] ATM Forum. (June 1, 1992). *ATM user-network interface specification, Version 2.0.*

[ATM93a] ATM Forum. (August 5, 1993). *ATM user-network interface specification, Version 3.0.*

[ATM94a] ATM Forum. (March, 1994). *Education and training work group*, ATM Forum Ambassador's Program.

[ATM94b] ATM Forum. (July 21, 1994). *ATM user-network interface specification, Version 3.1.*

[ATT89a] (January, 1989). Observations of error characteristics of fiber optic transmission systems, CCITT SGXVIII, San Diego, CA.

[BELL82] Bellamy, J. (1982). *Digital Telephony*, New York, NY: John Wiley and Sons.

[BELL90a] (May, 1993). Generic requirements for frame relay PVC exchange service, TR-TSV-001369, Issue 1.

[BELL89a]. (September, 1989). Synchronous optical network (SONET) transport systems: common generic criteria, TR-TSY-000253, Issue 1.

[BELL94] Bellman, R.B. (1994). Evolving traditional LANs to ATM, *Business Communications Review*, October.

[BLAC89] Black, U. (1989). *Data Networks, Concepts, Theory and Practice*, Prentice Hall.

[BLAC91] Black, U. (1991). *X.25 and related protocols*, IEEE Computer Society Press.

[BLAC93] Black, U. (1993). *Data link protocols*, Prentice Hall.

[BLAI88] Blair, C. (1988). SLIPs: Definitions, causes, and effects in T1 networks, *A Tautron Application Note, Issue 1*, September. (Note: my thanks to this author for a lucid explanation of slips.)

[BNR92a] Bell Northern Research. (1992). Global systems for mobile communications, *Telesis*, 92.

[BNR94a] Discussions held with Bell Northern Research (BNR) designers during 1993 and 1994.

[BROW94] Brown, P.D. (ed.). (1994). The price is right for ATM to become a serious competitor, *Broadband Networking News*, May.

[CCIT90a] (1990). Voice packetization-packetized voice protocols, CCITT Recommendation G.764, Geneva.

[CDPD93] (July 19, 1993). Cellular digital packet data system specification, *Release 1.0*.

[CHER92] Cherukuri, R. (August 26, 1992). Voice over frame relay networks, A technical paper issued as Frame Relay Forum, FRF 92.33.

[CHEU92] Cheung, N.K. (1992). The infrastructure of gigabit computer networks, *IEEE Communications Magazine*, April,.

[COMM94a] Korostoff, K. (April 18, 1994). Wide-area ATM undergoes trial by MAGIC, *Communications Week*.

[DAVI91] Davidson, R.P., and Muller, N.J. (1991). *The Guide to SONET*, Telecom Library, Inc.

[DELL92] Dell Computer, Intel, and University of Pennsylvania, A study compiled by Marty Baumann, *USA Today*, date not available.

[dePr91] dePrycker, M. (1991). *Asynchronous Transfer Mode*. Ellis Harwood Ltd.

[dePR92] de Prycker, M. (1992) ATM in Belgian Trial. *Communications International*, June.

[DUBO94] DuBois, D. Simnet Inc., Palo Alto, CA. A recommendation from a reviewer of *Emerging Communications Technologies*. (Thank you Mr. DuBois.)

[ECKB92] Eckberg, A.E. (1992). B-ISDN/ATM traffic and congestion control, *IEEE Network*, September.

[EMLI 63] Emling, J.W., and Mitchell, D. (1963). The effects of time delay and echoes on telephone conversations. *Bell Systems Technical Journal*, November.

[FORD93] Ford, P.S., Rekhter, Y., and Braun, H.-W. (1993). Improving the routing and addressing of IP. *IEEE Network*, May.

[FORU92] Frame Relay Forum Technical Committee. (May 7, 1992). "Frame relay network-to-network interface, phase 1 implementation agreement, Document Number FRF 92.08R1–Draft 1.4.

[GASM93] Gasman, L. (1993). ATM CPE—Who is providing what?, *Business Communications Review*, October.

[GOKE73] Goke, L.R., and Lipovski, G.J. (1973). Banyan networks for partitioning multiprocessor systems. First Annual Symposium on Computer Architecture.

[GRIL93] Grillo, D., MacNamee, R.J.G., and Rashidzadeh, B. (1993). Towards third generation mobile systems: A European possible transition path. *Computer Networks and ISDN Systems*, 25(8).

[GRON92] Gronert, E. (1992). MANS make their mark in Germany. *Data Communications International*, May.

[HAFN94] Hafner, K. (1994). Making sense of the internet. *Newsweek*, October 24.

[HALL92] Hall, M. (ed.). (1992). LAN-based ATM products ready to roll out. *LAN Technology*, September.

[HAND91] Handel, R., and Huber, M.N. (1991). *Integrated broadband networks: An introduction to ATM-based networks*. Addison-Wesley.

[HERM93] Herman, J., and Serjak C. (1993). ATM switches and hubs lead the way to a new era of switched internetworks. *Data Communications*, March.

[HEWL91] Hewlett Packard, Inc. (1991). Introduction to SONET, A tutorial.

[HEWL92] Hewlett Packard, Inc. (1992). Introduction to SONET networks and tests, An internal document.

[HEYW93] Heywood, P. (1993). PTTs gear up to offer high-speed services. *Data Communications*, August.

[HILL91] SONET, An overview. A paper prepared by Hill Associates, Inc., Winooski, VT, 05404.

[HUNT92] Hunter, P. (1992). What price progress?, *Communications International*, June.

[ITU93a] ITU-TS (1993). ITU-TS draft recommendation Q93.B "B-ISDN user-network interface layer 3 specification for basic call/bearer control. May.

[JAYA81] Jayant, N.S., and Christensen, S.W. (1981). Effects of packet losses on waveform-coded speech and improvements due to an odd-even interpolation procedure. *IEEE Transactions of Communications*, February.

[JOHN91] Johnson, J.T. (1991). Frame relay mux meets cell relay switch. *Data Communications*, October.

[JOHN92] Johnson, J.T. (1992). "Getting access to ATM. *Data Communications LAN Interconnect*, September 21.

[KING94] King, S.S. (1994). Switched virtual networks. *Data Communications*, September.

[KITA91] Kitawaki, N., and Itoh, K. (1991). Pure delay effects of speech quality in telecommunications. *IEEE Journal of Selected Areas in Communications*, May.

[LEE89] Lee, W.C.Y. (1989). *Mobile cellular telecommunications systems*. McGraw-Hill.

[LEE93] Lee, B.G., Kang, M., and Lee, J. (1993). *Broadband telecommunications technology*. Artech House.

[LISO91] Lisowski, B. (1991). Frame relay: what it is and how it works. *A Guide to Frame Relay, Supplement to Business Conmunications Review*, October.

[LIZZ94] Lizzio, J.R. (1994). Real-time RAID stokrage: the enabling technology for video-on-demand. *Telephony*, May 23.

[LYLE92] Lyles, J.B., and Swinehart, D.C. (1992). The emerging gigabit environment and the role of the local ATM. *IEEE Communications Magazine*, April.

[McCO94] McCoy, E. (1994). SONET, ATM and other broadband technologies. TRA Document # ATL72 16.9100, *Telecommunications Research Associates*, St. Marys, KS.

[MCQU91] McQuillan, J.M. (1991). Cell relay switching. *Data Communications*, September.

[MINO93] Minoli D. (1993). Proposed Cell Relay Bearer Service Stage 1 Description, T1S1.1/93-136 (Revision 1), ANSI Committee T1 (T1S1.1), June.

[MORE9] Moreney, J. (1994). ATM switch decision can wait, *Network World*, September 19.

[NOLL91] Nolle, T. (1991). Frame relay: Standards advance, *Business Communications Review*, October.

[NORT94] Northern Telecom. (1994). Consultant Bulletin 63020.16/02-94, Issue 1, February.

[[NYQU24] Nyquist, H. (1924). Certain factors affecting telegraph speed. *Transactions A.I.E.E.*

[PERL85] Perlman, R. (1985). An algorithm for distributed computation of spanning tree in an extended LAN. *Computer Communications Review, 15*(4) September.

[ROSE92] Rosenberry, W., Kenney D., and Fisher, G. (1992). *Understanding DCE.* O'Reilly & Associates.

[SALA92] Salamone, S. (1992). Sizing up the most critical issues. *Network World.*

[SAND94] Sandberg, J. (1994). Networking. *Wall Street Journal*, November 14.

[SHAN48] Shannon, C. (1948). Mathematical theory of communication, *Bell System Technical Journal, 27,* July and October.

[SRIR90a] Sriram, K. (1990a). Dynamic bandwidth allocation and congestion control schemes for voice and data integration in wideband packet technology, *Proc. IEEE. Supercomm/ICC '90, 3,* April.

[SRIR90b] Sriram, K. (1990b). Bandwidth allocation and congestion control scheme for an integrated voice and data network. *US Patent No. 4, 914650,* April 3.

[SRIR93a] Sriram, K. (1993). Methodologies for bandwidth allocation, transmission scheduling, and congestion avoidance in broadband ATM networks. *Computer Networks and ISDN Systems, 26*(1), September.

[SRIR93b] Sriram, K., and Lucantoni, D.M. (1993). Traffic smoothing effects of bit dropping in a packet voice multiplexer. *IEEE Transactions on Communications*, July.

[STEW92] Steward, S.P. (1992). The world report '92. *Cellular Business*, May.

[WADA89] Wada, M. (1989). Selective recovery of video packet loss using error concelment. *IEEE Journal of Selected Areas in Communications*, June.

[WALL91] Wallace, B. (1991). Citicorp goes SONET. *Network World*, November 18.

[WERK92] Wernik, M., Aboul-Magd, O., and Gilber, H. (1992). Traffic management for B-ISDN services. *IEEE Network*, September.

[WEST92] Westgate, J. (1992).*OSI Management*, NCC Blackwell.

[WILL92] Williamson, J. (1992). GSM bids for global recognition in a crowded cellular world. *Telephony*, April 6.

[WU93] Wu, T.-H. (1993). Cost-effective network evolution. *IEEE Communications Magazine*, September.

[YAP93] Yap, M.-T., and Hutchison (1993). An emulator for evaluating DQDB performance. *Computer Networks and ISDN Systems, 25*(11).

[YOKO93] Yokotani, T., Sato, H., and Nakatsuka, S. (1993). A study on a performance improvement algorithm in DQDB MAN. *Computer Networks and ISDN Systems, 25*(10).

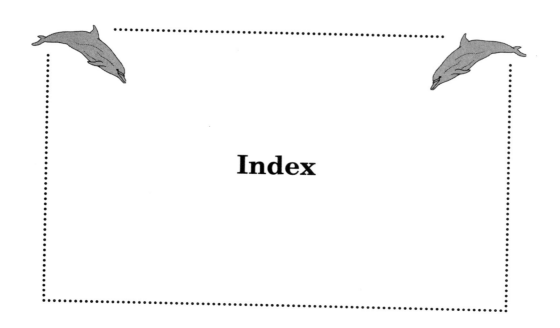

Index

AAL common part (AAL CP), 18
AAL, closer look at, 34–38
  formats of AAL PDUs, 36–38
Addressing, SAPs, primitives, and PDUs,
    50–63
  ATM address scheme, 52–55
  ATM's use of OSI Model, 61
  broadband signaling stacks and the user
    layers, 61–63
  connection mapping, 58–60
  E.164 address scheme, 55–56
  explicit addresses and labels, 50–51
  other key concepts, 60–61
  routing, 51–52
  service access points (SAPs), 56–58
ANSI T1.648, 113
Asynchronous Transfer Mode (ATM), 24
AT&T, 40
ATM
  introduction to, 1–7
    broadband signaling networks, 6–7
    narrowband transport and signaling
      networks, 3–6
    signaling system, purpose of, 1–2
    SS7, 7
    transport systems and signaling
      systems, 2–3
ATM Adaptation Layer (AAL), 17
ATM address scheme, 52–55
  authority format identifier (AFI), 52

  domain specific part (DSP), 52
  initial domain part (IDP), 52
  initial donain identifier (IDI), 52
ATM architecture, 24–38
  AAL, closer look at, 34–38
  and B-ISDN, 26–27
  ATM cell and cell header, 32–34
  ATM layers, 27–29
  overview of, 24–25
  virtual circuits with VPCI, VPI, VCI,
    29–32
ATM cell and cell header, 32–34
ATM connection control messages, table, 95
ATM Forum, 159
  UNI Signaling Specification (version
    4.0), 92
ATM layers, 27–29
ATM Local Management Interface (LMI),
    18
*ATM: Foundation for Broadband
    Networks,* 5
Automated calling card service (ACCS), 48

B-ISDN
  and ATM, 26–27
  definition of, 14–16
  functional entities and reference points,
    16–18
    B-ISDN planes and layers, 16–18
  layers, major functions of, 18–21

B-ISUP interfaces, primitives, and
        primitive parameters, 139–143
B-ISUP messages, 120–123
    table, 120
B-ISUP signaling, 113–143
    B-ISUP architecture in more detail,
        127–131
    B-ISUP interfaces, primitives, and
        primitive parameters, 139–143
    B-ISUP NNI messages and parameters,
        119–123
    B-ISUP operations, examples of,
        123–127
    B-ISUP operations, overview of, 117–119
        setting up virtual circuits, 119
        trunk groups and VPCIs, 118
    B-ISUP, purpose of, 114
    parameters used in B-ISUP messages,
        131–138
    position of B-ISUP in broadband
        signaling layers, 116
    SS7 MTP support to B-ISUP, 116–117
    what B-ISUP does not do, 114–116
        bandwidth analysis and path
            discovery, 115–116
B-ISUP timers, table, 125–126
Backward direction, 162
Bellcore GR-1431-CORE, 152
Bellcore GR-2878-CORE, 68
Bellcore RR-1417-CORE, 155
Broadband ISDN (B-ISDN), 8
Broadband services, classification of,
        21–23
Broadband signaling networks, 6–7
Broadband signaling operations and
        performance requirements, 148–158
    configuration options, 148–151
    performance requirements for signaling
        virtual channel connection (VCC),
        155–157
    point-to-multipoint calls, 152
    signaling identifiers (SIDs), 152–155
        add party operations, 154–155
Broadband signaling stacks, 92–93
    and other user layers, 61–63
Broadband switching system (BSS), 148

Cell delay variation tolerance (CDVT) at
        UNI, table, 157
Cell loss priority (C) field, 34
Common Channel Interoffice Signaling
        (CCIS), 40
Common channel signaling, 40

CONNECT–ANM mapping, table, 146
Connection mapping, 58–60
Country code (CC), 55
Crankback, 161

E.164 address scheme, 55–56
Enhanced 800 (E800) services, 48
Error codes, 79

File Transfer Protocol (FTP), 18
Forward direction, 162
Fractional T1, 12

Generic flow control (GFC) field, 32

Header error control (HEC) field, 34
Hello, 162, 172

Information service elements, functions of,
        table, 96
Integrated Services Digital Network
        (ISDN), 3, 8
International Telecommunications Union-
        Telecommunication Standardization
        Sector (ITU-T), 4
Internet RFC 1695, 114
Internet Simple Network Management
        Protocol (SNMP), 18
ISDN and B-ISDN architecture, 8–23
    B-ISDN functional entities and reference
        points, 16–18
        B-ISDN planes and layers, 16–18
    B-ISDN, definition of, 14–16
    clasification of broadband services,
        21–23
    interfaces and functional groupings,
        8–11
        reference points, 10–11
    ISDN configuration, typical, 12–13
    ISDN layers, 13–14
    ISDN logical channel concept, 11–12
    layers, major functions of, 18–21
*ISDN and SS7: Architectures for Digital
        Signaling Networks*, 151
*ISDN and SS7: Foundation for Digital
        Signaling Networks,* 8
ISDN configuration, typical, 12–13
ISDN layers, 13–14
ISO 8348, 52
ITU-T Q.2764 and Q.2763, 113
ITU-T Recommendation E.164, 55
ITU-T Recommendation I.211, 21
ITU-T Recommendation I.321, 18

ITU-T Recommendation Q.2144, 68
ITU-T Recommendation Q.2931, 92
ITU-T Recommendation X.213, 52

Lee, Whay C., 167
Link metrics, 161
Logical channel number (LCN), 51
Logical link, 162

Mapping at AP and ASE interfaces, table,
    129
Mapping of primitives and B-ISUP
    messages, table, 130

Narrowband transport and signaling
    networks, 3–6
  T1 system, 3–4
  X.25 and packet switching systems, 4–6

Operations between UNI and NNI,
    144–147
  mapping between UNI and NNI
    messages and information elements,
    147
  typical call setup and release operations,
    144–147
Operations, administration, and
    maintenance (OAM), 60
OSI Common Management Information
    Protocol (CMIP), 18
OSI Model, 13–14, 29, 41, 44, 50, 58, 71,
    127
  ATM's use of, 61

Parameters used in B-ISUP messages,
    131–138
Payload type identifier (PTI) field, 34
PCR values to be supported by equivalent
    bandwidth, table, 156
Peleg, David, 167
Per-trunk, in-band signaling, 39
Permissible modifications, table, 177
PNNI messages for call and connection
    control (point-to-point), table, 176
PNNI topology state parameters (PTSEs),
    170
Point codes (PCs), 47
Preceding network, 162
Preceding side, 162
Primitives and parameters
  at (b) interface, table, 139
  at (c) interface, table, 140
  at (d) interface, table, 141–142

  at (e) interface, table, 143
  at (f) interface, table, 143
Primitives between SSCF and MTP3,
    table, 74
Private network-network interface (PNNI),
    159–180
  designated transit list (DTL), 178
  horizontal and outside links, 171–172
  information elements to support other
    services, 179
  NNI protocol, overview of, 160–161
  NNI protocol, reason for, 159–160
  PNNI hierarchy example, 172–174
  PNNI metrics, 165–171
    metric aggregation, 167–171
  PNNI signaling messages, 175–178
    PNNI available bit rate (ABR)
      descriptors, 177–178
    SETUP message information
      elements, 175–177
  PNNI signaling specification model,
    162–163
  PNNI signaling, unique aspects of and
    Q.2931, 161–162
  soft permanent virtual connection
    procedures, 178–179
    crankback, 179
    designated transit list, 179
  terms and concepts, 163–165

Q.2931 protocol, 18
Q.931 message information elements,
    106–112
  AAL information element, 107–109
    AAL type 1, 107–109
    AAL type 3/4, 109
  broadband low-layer information
    element, 109–112
Quality of service (QOS), 2, 165

Reference points, ISDN, 10–11
RELEASE–REL mapping, table, 147
Retricted transit node, 161
Routing, 51–52
Routing control channel, 161

SAAL entities and MTP3, relationships of
    parameters in primitives and PDUs,
    90–91
SAAL, SSCOP, and SSCF, 64–91
  error codes, 79
  position of SAAL in broadband signaling
    layers, 64–66

SAAL, SSCOP, and SSCF *(cont.)*
  position of SAAL in broadband signaling
    layers *(cont.)*
    protocol stack in more detail, 65–66
  SAAL entities and MTP3, relationships
    of, 89–91
    parameters in the primitives and
      PDUs, 90–91
  SAAL primitives and signals operations,
    71–78
    depictions of layers and associated
      primitives and signals, 71
    primitives and signals between SSCF
      and MTP3, 71–75
    signals between layer management
      and SSCF, 77–78
    signals between SSCOP-SSCF and
      SSCOP-layer management, 75–77
  SAAL, functions of, 67–71
    SSCF, functions of, 67–69
    SSCOP, functions of, 69–70
    SSCS layer management (LM),
      functions of, 70–71
  signals between SSCOP and CPCS,
    78–79
  SSCOP operations in more detail,
    79–89
    SSCOP housekeeping operations,
      examples of, 83–84
    SSCOP PDUs, 80–83
    SSCOP transferring signaling traffic,
      examples of, 84–89
Schaffer, Alejandro A., 167
Service access points (SAPs), 50, 56–58
  primitives, functions of, table, 58
  primitives, use of, 57–58
  relationships of service definitions and
    protocol specifications, 58
    protocol specfications, 58
    service definitions, 58
Service-specific connection-oriented
    protocol (SSCOP), 18, 64
Service-specific coordination function
    (SSCF), 64
SETUP–IAM mapping, table, 146
Signaling ATM adaptation layer (SAAL),
    17, 64
Signaling System Number 7 (SS7), see also
    SS7, 39–49
Signaling systems
  purpose of, 1–2
  transport systems and, 2–3

Signals between layer management and
    SCCP, table, 78
Signals between SSCF and SSCOP and
    SSCOP and layer management,
    table, 75
Signals between SSCOP and CPCS, table,
    79
SS7, 7
SS7 architecture, 39–49
  common channel signaling, 40
  fundamentals, 40–41
  history of signaling, 39
  identifiers and numbering scheme, 47–49
  nodes, functions of, 41–47
  topology, example of, 41
SS7 identifiers and numbering scheme,
    47–49
  global title addressing and translation,
    49
SS7 nodes, functions of, 41–47
  levels (layers)
    ISDN user part (ISUP), 45
    message transfer part (MTP), 44–45
    MTP levels, 45–46
    remote operations service element
      (ROSE), 46
    signaling connection control point
      (SCCP), 45
    transaction capabilities application
      part (TCAP), 46, 47
  service control point (SCP), 43–44
  service switching point (SSP), 43
  signaling transfer point (STP), 43
SS7 topology, example of, 41
SSCF, functions of, 67–69
  alignment procedures, 68
  flow control, 67
  layer management, 67
  link status, 67
  proving algorithm, 68–69
  SSCF PDU, 69
SSCOP list, table, 84
SSCOP operations in more detail, 79–89
  SSCOP housekeeping operations,
    examples of, 83–84
    relationship of SSCF/SSCOP
      primitives and SSCOP PDUs, 83–84
  SSCOP PDUs, 80–83
  SSCOP transferring signaling traffic,
    84–89
SSCOP protocol data units (PDUs),
    summary of, table, 81

SSCOP, functions of, 69–70
  SSCOP and AAL5, 69–70
SSCS layer management (LM), functions
    of, 70–71
Succeeding network, 162
Sustained cell rate (SCR) and equivalent
    bandwidth, 157
Synchronous Optical Network (SONET), 2

T1, 3–4
Time division multiplexing (TDM), 11
Timers, table, 99
Topology state parameters, 162
Transmission Control Protocol/Internet
    Protocol (TCP-IP), 18
Transport systems
  and signaling systems, 2–3
    blurring of distinction between, 3
Type of service factors (TOS), 165

U.S. Bell System, 3
UNI messages and information elements,
    93–95
UNI operations, 100–106
  add party operation, 103–106
  connection establishment operation,
    100–101
  connection release operation, 101–102
  drop party operation, 103–106
  overview, 95–99
  restart operation, 102–103
  status inquiry operation, 103
UNI signaling, 92–112
  ATM form UNI version 4.0 variations,
    112

broadband signaling stacks, 92–93
Q.931 message information elements, in
  more detail, 106–112
UNI messages and information
  elements, 93–95
  information elements, 95
  message format, 94
  the messages, 95
UNI operations, in more detail, 100–106
  add party operation, 103–106
  connection establishment operation,
    100–101
  connection release operation, 101–102
  drop party operation, 106
  restart operation, 102–103
  status inquiry operation, 103
UNI operations, overview, 95–99
  Q.2931 timers, 98–99
User network interface (UNI) protocol, 8

Virtual channel identifier (VCI), 29
Virtual circuit identifier (VCI), 51
Virtual circuits
  with VPCI, VPI, VCI, 29–32
Virtual path connection identifier (VPCI),
    32
Virtual path identifier (VPI), 29

X.25 and packet switching systems, 4
  fixed and variable length messsages, 5
  inband and out-of-band signaling, 5
  problems with narrowband signaling, 6
  SS7 systems, 6
  virtual circuit concept, 5
X.25 specification, 4